1,000 MORE CELTIC QUOTES, NOTES AND ANECDOTES

Volume 2

Robert Harvey

The cover of this book was designed by 147 Enterprises, Hamilton, 01698 282178

Thank You to Johnny Mullaney from the Brisbane Celtic Supporters Club for
permission to use the picture on the back page. See www.brisbanecsc.com

Order this book online at www.trafford.com/
or email orders@trafford.com

Most Trafford titles are also available at major online book retailers.

Printed in Victoria, BC, Canada.

ISBN: 978-1-4269-1989-3

*Our mission is to efficiently provide the world's finest, most comprehensive
book publishing service, enabling every author to experience success.
To find out how to publish your book, your way, and have it available
worldwide, visit us online at www.trafford.com/*

www.trafford.com

North America & international
toll-free: 1 888 232 4444 (USA & Canada)
phone: 250 383 6864 ✦ fax: 812 355 4082

This book is dedicated to my Dad, **Robert Harvey**
(1927-2008)

He took me to my first Celtic game. Thank You for showing me that football should always be exciting and always played in a good spirit.

Dad had no time for players who feigned injury, or made square passes, or passed the ball backwards. It was not the Celtic way. He liked to see players play with a smile, and not moaning all the time. He liked to see players go forward and beat a man. He liked to see players who were comfortable no matter if the ball came to their left foot or right foot. He liked to sit with his bottle of Guinness in the kitchen every day and read the sports pages: Guinness, football, and horse racing was his perfect afternoon.

Dad passed on his love of Celtic to my brother Gerry and me. I still remember him celebrating the night Celtic won the European Cup in 1967, and my young brother (who was 7 years old) standing in the corner with the TV aerial to make sure we got a good picture on the old four-legged black and white telly.

Dad watched Celtic from the 1930's. Some of his favourite players were Bobby Hogg, Jimmy Delaney, Bobby Evans, Bobby Murdoch, Jimmy Johnstone, Kenny Dalglish, Brian McClair, Paul McStay, Naka-mura, Aidan McGeady – he always thought the brave players were the ones who took the kicks, got up, and just got on with game.

OTHER BOOKS BY ROBERT HARVEY

" 1,000 Quotes, Notes and Anecdotes ". This is a collection from players and managers from different teams around the world.

" 1,000 Celtic Quotes, Note, and Anecdotes ". This was the first collection of Celtic quotes.

INTRODUCTION:

Welcome to the second volume of **Celtic Quotes, Notes and Anecdotes**, especially if you are Celtic daft. Every Celtic supporter has a favourite story to tell or a favourite quote.

When I was growing up in Fernhill near Rutherglen, the days were spent eating, sleeping, talking, and playing football. In the distance I could often see the towering flood lights high above Celtic Park, and on a clear night if the wind was blowing in the right direction, you could hear the roar of the crowd from the big European Cup games. I used to wonder what magical games must have been played at Celtic Park.

I am very lucky that I live only a 20 minutes walk from Celtic Park and for many years now I have been to all the home games. Our seats are just at the tunnel where the players come onto the park. You get to know familiar faces of the supporters all around you. For years we have had some "elderly " great guys sitting next to us who can recall the Exhibition Cup, the Coronation Cup, the 7-1 victory in 1957 against Rangers, the European Cup Final, and many other great games and the great players. They love Celtic and have followed them through good times and bad times, and tell wonderful little stories that only a real supporter would remember and tell. Celtic Park is full of people who all have their own wonderful story to tell. We should never worry about repeating old quotes or anecdotes. There is always a new generation around who have never heard them before. It is passing on your little bit of the Celtic history.

I hope you enjoy this collection of quotes and anecdotes. Many of them will stick in your mind for a long time. Some of them will make you laugh, some of them may take you back in time to a game that were at, some of them may surprise you, some of them may remind you of the great players who have helped create the history of Celtic.

Like any collection of this type, some of the quotes and stories may be inaccurate, exaggerated, or have become a myth through time. If you wish to have any of these changed for a future edition please email me at **glasgowquotes@yahoo.co.uk**

Finally, if you are interested in contributing a story or quote to a future edition, I would love to hear from you. Every Celtic supporter has a story to tell.

Robert Harvey
www.celticquotes.co.uk

Europe, Asia, North and South America, Australia, the Middle East and Africa, The Pacific
23 September 2009

THOUGHTS OF A CELTIC SUPPORTER

Aisling Kane (Claddagh C.S.C. Galway) gives her thoughts on what supporting Celtic means to her:

"Let me try and sum up the true meaning of supporting Celtic Football Club. To me they mean more than football, they are family. Apart from my marriage and the birth of my little Bhoy (God Jnr), Seville has been the greatest and most treasured memory I have experienced in my life so far and that includes receiving numerous degrees and career promotions.

As I stood there with my mam, dad, brothers, husband and my little Bhoy among 80,000 plus Celtic supporters in the roaring heat of 40°C in Seville that day I realised what supporting Celtic was all about. Those magical moments in Seville is what possesses so many of us to travel week in and week out spending money and many hours travelling to sit in the rain and support Celtic regardless of whom they are playing. Something magical happened that day in Seville to every Celtic fan around the world that no amount of trophies could ever achieve. We were all so proud of how well our beloved Celtic played and how well our fans supported them. That day Celtic gained recognition from around the world that not only were they a world class team but also that they had the best supporters in the world.

That puts a meaning to me on why I have supported them since I was a young girl and why I spend so many hours travelling to see them. It is in our blood and we all live and breathe Celtic as they are not just about football, they are about family and everyone knows you would do anything in the world for your family. Celtic Football Club is the biggest and proudest family in the world." Once again the passports will be dusted down for another European trip to Teplice in March. That aside, the association is making plans for trip to Las Vegas in the summer to meet up with their friends in the North American Federation of Celtic Supporters Clubs for their bi-annual Convention, not to mention Celtic's proposed tour of the USA. It's a tough life being a Celt!! www.aicsc.com/celticviewarticles2.html#vol38iss3

EVERY CELTIC SUPPORTER HAS A STORY TO TELL.

Every Celtic supporter has a story to tell. For generations families have sat round the fireplace at night listening to their Dad or Grand Father talking about the great Celtic games, players, and their favourite memories.

Recently I set up a website called www.celticquotes.co.uk for Celtic quotes and stories.

Already Celtic supporters in places as far away as South Africa and Australia have contributed some magical stories. For example, see story number 7 on the website from the Civil War in Burundi, Africa. Only a Celtic supporter could tell this story! Many of the stories will stick in your mind for a long time.

If you are interested in contributing a story or quote, I would love to hear from you.

Do not worry about repeating old stories. There is always a new generation around who have never heard them before.

Here are a few things that may help:

1. **Go to www.celticquotes.co.uk and you can send via the home page.** This also enables you to see the experiences and stories that other Celtic supporters across the world have posted. This is an excellent place to start.
2. **Be positive**. - promote everything that is good about Celtic.
3. **Be international**. Celtic is a global club with supporters everywhere.
4. **Be brief** (if you want). A simple quote can paint a wonderful picture. A few years ago I compiled a book called " **1,000 Celtic Quotes, Notes, and Anecdotes**." My favourite quote

throughout the history of Celtic was by Willie Maley : "It is not his creed or his nationality that counts, it is the man himself."

5. You do not need to be Shakespeare. Everyone has their own unique, funny, or hair-raising story to tell. It can be as short or as long as you want.

6. **Be Happy.** You are a Celtic supporter !

7. **Spread the word:** If one of the stories or quotes puts a smile on your face, please pass it on to your friends, family, or work colleagues who support the Glasgow Celtic.

If you need any further information I can be contacted via email at glasgowquotes@yahoo.co.uk

1. **" Records can be broken, but History cannot be changed."** On May 25th, 1967, Celtic made History when they became the first British club to win the European Champions Cup.

2. It has always been our ambition to represent all that is best in this great game. Celtic chairman **Robert Kelly** at the end of the season in 1967

3. He is the most honest footballer I have ever known. England Word Cup winner Jack Charlton talking about **Bobby Murdoch**

4. He has brought happiness to thousands of people across the world. **Ellen Harvey** talking outside Celtic Park in July 2009 at the statue of Brother Walfrid

5. He must have spent a considerable period near the Blarney Stone in his youth, as his persuasive powers once experienced were never forgotten. Celtic manager Willie Maley talking about **Brother Walfrid**

6. Cups are not won by individuals. They are won by men in a team, men who put their club before personal prestige. I am lucky – I have the players who do just that for Celtic. **Jock Stein** two days before the European Cup Final in Lisbon

7. " The Manager of the Century." Brian Clough manager of Nottingham Forest, describes **Jock Stein** in a telegram he sent to Jock at his testimonial dinner in the banqueting hall at Glasgow City Chambers.

8. The chase is over. This proves that the Old Firm are not infirm. Congratulations on winning the league. Best of luck in Europe next year. Rangers vice chairman John Wilson sent a telegram to Celtic chairman **Bob Kelly** after Celtic won the league in 1966. Little did he know that 9-in-a-row was about to happen.

9.   He gave me my dreams. **Billy McNeill** talking about Celtic manager Jock Stein

10.   The Lisbon Lions used to play the reserves (the Quality Street Gang) in training games. The reserve team was an exceptional group of young players including Lou Macari, George Connelly, Davie Hay, Danny McGrain, Kenny Dalglish, Davie Cattenach, Paul Wilson, John Gorman, Jimmy Quinn, and Vic Davidson. These games were serious stuff and better than many Premier league games. If **Jock Stein** was the referee then the Lions would always win: if his assistant **Sean Fallon** was the referee then the reserves had a chance.

11.   I am now going to tell him (Herrera) how Celtic will be the first team to bring the European Cup back to Britain. But it will not help him in any manner, shape or form: we are going to attack as we have never attacked before. **Jock Stein** before the Lisbon Cup Final

12.   " **From Desperation, came Celebration**." Banner at the Celtic versus Hibs game at Celtic Park in May 2008.

13.   People told me, 'It was going in anyway', but it had more chance of going for a throw-in. Steve (Chalmers) got a great touch to turn it in." **Bobby Murdoch** talking about the greatest goal in Celtic's history – the winner in the European Cup Final. Bobby had been protecting his right foot, having injured it early in the game, and opted to strike Tommy Gemmell's cutback with his weaker left. Chalmers's deft touch put his name in the history books as scorer, and the modest Murdoch never sought credit.

14.   I wish he (Patsy Gallacher) had been captured on film. He had the most perfect balance. Celtic chairman **Sir Robert Kelly** talking about the greatest player he had ever seen.

15. **Patsy Gallacher** was the star of Celtic team in the early 1900's. He was a "part time" player. He used to leave Celtic Park in the early afternoon and go and manage his wine and spirits business! Manager Willie Maley was not happy with this, but didn't stop Patsy.

16. "Parkheid is no place for a footballer looking for a job". **Peter Somers** who played inside left during the great Celtic winning teams between 1905-1910. Peter was one of those players who " never lost his head in defeat or victory." He was always cheery.

17. When **Fergus McCann** was building the new stadium, all the local residents were complaining that their TV reception was impaired. Fergus agreed to pay for new aerials, if the residents of Stamford Road would appear at Celtic Park the next day with their TV licences to prove that they lived there. No one turned up

18. Once the UEFA Cup Final went into extra-time, I bet there wasn't a football fan in Britain - with the possible exception of some Rangers followers - who weren't rooting for Celtic. They had the whole country on their side and that in itself is an achievement. My abiding memory, however, is of the fans who sang `You'll Never Walk Alone' on the final whistle. It was one of the most emotional sights and sounds I've ever witnessed inside a football stadium. **Rodney Marsh**, Sky TV sports pundit talking about the Celtic fans in Seville after the UEFA Cup Final against Porto.

19. "An Gorta Mor – One Million dead, Three Million Dispersed, The Descendants remember." Banner at the Celtic versus Hibs game at Celtic Park in May 2008. The Great Famine (An Gorta Mor) happened between 1845-1851.

20. The supporters are great at Celtic Park. There is never any trouble, even during the derby games. People in Scotland prefer to

drink beer or eat a piece and sausage. **Artur Boruc.** (Translated from Polish so may not be wholly accurate!)

21. "YOU MUST GET excited at football. If there is no excitement, there's no game." **Felicia Grant** who in the 1960's was the largest shareholder at Celtic. She never saw Celtic play, but always followed the team's progress. She had a big picture of John Thomson on her mantelpiece.

22. I WILL NEVER forget what Billy McNeill told me about the job of a Celtic captain. That is never to be seen to hang your head. If a skipper is playing badly he must see that it does **not** affect his team mates. **Roy Aitken.**

23. NOWADAYS AT HALF time players are eating chocolate and sugary drinks because sports scientists say it is good for them. When I played after training we would nip along to Joe's Kitchen at Parkhead Cross and eat sausage, bacon and eggs. As an alternative we would eat soup and a plate of chips and wash it all down with milkshakes. So it is all change today. Celtic coach **Tommy Burns** speaking in the summer of 2007.

24. WHEN I WAS a kid I remember I used to love the Celtic jersey. Italian star **Gianluca Zambrotta** who played full back for Juventus and Barcelona recalls his affection for the famous Hoops jersey.

25. WHEN CELTIC WERE preparing at Seamill for the European Cup final in 1967, Jock Stein and his players watched the tape of the greatest football game ever played, the 1960 European Cup Final when Real Madrid beat Eintracht Frankfurt 7-3 at Hampden. When you watch beautiful games, you get beautiful ideas. Big Jock wanted his players to play with the attacking spirit of Real Madrid. **Pub football expert**

26. " HERE LIES Gordon Strachan. At least it is better than Bratislava."
Gordon Strachan used to joke about the words that would be
on his gravestone. His first competitive game as manager of Celtic
was the 5-0 defeat by Artmedia Bratislava in the Champions league
game in July 2005.

27. IF THAT MATCH had been written for Roy of the Rovers, no one
would believe it. Thank God for players, they never cease to amaze
me. Celtic manager **Billy McNeill** after Celtic beat Rangers 4-2
to win the league in May 1979

28. THERE IS AN ingredient about this club that you can't quite put into
words. I think it goes back to the very early days. I think it was
founded for the right reasons and I think those reasons have stayed
with us. **Billy McNeill**

29. "MANY VOICES THAT can still remember the past may, by then,
have lapsed into silence." Celtic chairman **Desmond White** explains why Celtic decided to have an official history produced 10
years before the Centenary year.

30. WHEN TEACHERS ASKED us in class what we wanted to be, the
other kids would say the obvious things like a train driver, or a
fireman. I always said I wanted to be a professional footballer.
Henrik Larsson.

31. I AM PLEASED and honoured to present this award because of the
extraordinary behaviour before, during, and after the UEFA cup
final in Seville. They behaved as football fans should and we would
never have any violence or trouble at matches if all fans behaved
that way. They reacted as if they had won the game and they
mingled with the winners which was wonderful. This is football
and it is easy to win, but it is not so easy to lose. FIFA President
Sepp Blatter presents the Fair Play Award to Celtic supporters.

32.   THE MAN WITH fire in his eyes. **Dermot Desmond's** description
      of manager Martin O'Neill

33.   A PIECE OF Celtic history will take place at Barrowfield on Sunday
      12/08/2007 when the Celtic Ladies team play their first ever com-
      petitive game. The Scottish Women's Premier League kicks off
      and **Celtic Ladies** face Hamilton Accies Ladies.

34.   OBVIOUSLY YOU CONSIDER the players who are in form, the players
      who have done well against continental teams, and you also add
      a dash of sentiment. I have been described sometimes as hard and
      ruthless, but when you forget sentiment in football you can find
      yourself on the slippery slope. **Jock Stein** describes how picks his
      team for vital European games.

35.   A TRAVELLER FROM Govan visited the famous Chatuchak market in
      Bangkok As he walked around he seen a sports stall selling football
      jerseys: Manchester United, AC Milan, Barcelona, Real Madrid,
      Celtic. He went across to the seller and asked, " Any Rangers
      taps?" The Thai salesman had a mouthful of Green Curry and
      replied without looking up, " No. Only sell big teams, only sell
      big teams"

36.   IF ANY CELTS fans are in Bangkok and want to watch the Celts
      in the Champions Leagure simply walk to the top of the Khao
      San Road (Opposite end from Gullivers). Directly behind Burger
      King there is a small bar (it has no name), which is open 24 hours.
      The local plod drink here so it can stay open all night and they
      will serve you drinks, albeit in tea mugs. If the Celtic game is on
      live they will put it on. Don't be shy about asking for the Celtic
      game. The owners are all from Laos, but they are Tims (Well they
      are after I gave one of them my Hoops jerseys). The Shamrock on
      Khao San will only show the game the staff are betting on, usually
      a game featuring an English club. Hail Hail, the Bangkok Bhoys.

37. YOU PEOPLE SOMETIMES are like those serial killers that you see in films who send out these horrible messages. The serial killer who cuts out the words 'I am going to get you' or 'Your wife is next '. Celtic manager **Gordon Strachan** told a media conference about how they manipulate the meaning of what players say.

38. WONDER DISPLAY KEEPS the League Cup at Parkhead; **JUST ONE WORD FOR CELTIC- MAGNIFICENT.** Headline in the Sunday Post newspaper on   20 October 1957. Celtic beat Rangers 7-1.

39. I NEVER THINK I am as good as Sir Alex Ferguson or Carlo Ancellotti at AC Milan. They can fantasise more than I can. All I can do is use what money I have. I would judge myself against these guys, but only if I had the same weapons. I wouldn't judge myself against you if I had a knife and you had a gun. **Gordon Strachan** talking about the transfer funds available to managers in the Champions league.

40. I THINK THE fans today, 40 years after Lisbon, recognise how close we all were (all the Lisbon Lions) to them, and we still are today. This is something that is difficult to achieve these days because of the salaries of football players. **Billy McNeill**.

41. I BRING SINCERE congratulations from the city of Glasgow to Celtic for providing Europe, and indeed the world, with the ideal of sportsmanship. **Lord Provost Peter McCann** speaking at the Glasgow City Hall in a tribute night to Celtic for winning 9 league championships in a row.

42. I'VE BEEN INTO photography in the last few years. I love getting out on my day off, going up the west coast to places like Invereray or Ardrishaig and taking pictures. Celtic manager **Gordon Strachan**

43. I WILL BE staying here as long as I am needed. We have been
     through a lot together in the last six glorious years and you don't
     break those links so easily. There is still much to do. **Jock Stein** in
     1971 after he turned down an offer to be manager of Manchester
     United

44. IN 2007 A couple from Glasgow took Celtic and Rangers football
     jerseys to an orphanage in Africa. Before the game against the
     Rangers boys, the Celtic boys did a Huddle!! Celtic won the
     game 3-0.

45. "HE IS THE bravest Sportsman in the world." World famous knee
     surgeon Dr.Richard Steadman in Colorado talking about Celtic's
     John Kennedy. Dr.Steadman has performed approx 10,000 knee
     operations in his career, including helping famous players like Del
     Piero, Ronaldo, Shearer and Larsson. John was seriously injured
     playing for Scotland against Romania at Hampden. He was the
     victim of a dreadful over the ball challenge. Dr.Steadman said it
     was the worst sports injury he had ever seen.

46. I REMEMBER THE atmosphere at Parkhead was one of the best ex-
     periences of my life. Our relationship with Celtic is very good,
     the directors are gentlemen and I am sure that will be reflected
     in the way the fans react. **Juan Laporta**, President of Barcelona.
     He was speaking before the Celtic versus Barcelona Champions
     league game in Glasgow when Henrik Larsson was returning to
     Celtic Park as a Barcelona player in September 2004.

47. WE WERE ON £65 a week when I played and I always say that if I
     was on £25,000 a week they could put boxes of tomatoes around
     the track and they could throw them at me if I had a bad game.
     That's the way I see it. **George Connelly** reflects on changing
     times and the pay of modern day players.

48. BEING CELTIC MANAGER and having the chance to take the club into
     the Champions League against Manchester United and AC Milan

gives me the opportunity to stand shoulder to shoulder with Sir Alex Ferguson or Carlo Ancelotti. I'll never forget Ancelotti's face as he watched the Celtic fans singing You'll Never Walk Alone before our meeting last season. He turned to look back at the people in his dugout and his expression was a mixture of disbelief and awe. That's why I love being the Celtic manager. **Gordon Strachan**.

49. **Jimmy McGrory** was often asked what was the best ever Celtic team? He picked the following players: John Thomson, Willie McStay, Peter McGonagle, Bobby Murdoch, Billy McNeill, George Paterson, Jimmy Delaney, Patsy Gallacher, Jimmy McGrory (Joe McBride), Joe Cassidy, Adam McLean.

50. The pace of the game at European Championship League level is frightening. One minute you're attacking and two seconds later they're in your own box and you have to make a 60 or 70 yard run to keep up with your man. **Scott Brown**.

51. When you travel away to Europe you are there almost 24 hours a day. **Davie Hay**.

52. " Not at all, it's better than digging ditches." **Bobby Lennox** answers a question from a journalist asking if he ever gets tired with the daily travelling from his home in Ayrshire to Celtic Park for training.

53. A little encouragement can go a long way. **It's hard to beat a person who never gives up.** That is the Celtic team spirit. Going to Celtic Park is not just a game of football, but an experience. **Pub football expert**

54. **Gordon Strachan's** first competitive game as manager of Celtic was the 5-0 defeat by Artmedia Bratislava. Oddly, his watch stopped working during that game. He had worn it for years without any problems, but it stopped that night.

55. WHEN YOU LEAVE Celtic, you leave home. **Willie Ferguson** who played outside left for Celtic between 1895 and 1897.

56. I MEAN HOW fast was their right winger ? At half time I almost had to give our left back, Lee Naylor, the phone number for the Samaritans. Celtic manager **Gordon Strachan** talking after the famous Celtic penalty shoot out win against Spartak Moscow in August 2007 at Celtic Park.

57. HE WAS BRILLIANT, he wasn't just skilful, he was a powerful little man, brave as a lion, and his fitness was remarkable. He was a very good goal scorer, he loved the adulation of the crowd, and he was a real Celtic man. **Billy McNeill** talking about Jimmy Johnstone

58. HE HAD A fantastic sense of humour. I felt that for the ability that he had and the status that he had, he was an amazingly humble man. Martin O'Neill talking about **Jimmy Johnstone**

59. BAD TEMPERED GLASGOW man interested in beer, cigarettes, curries and Glasgow Celtic Football Club, seeks nimble sex pot, preferably Asian, for long nights of screaming passion. Must have own car and be willing to travel to away games. Advert in a **Lonely Hearts** magazine.

60. IN 25 YEARS' time, when I'm on the golf course somewhere, this game will come back to me. It was the European tie that had everything and what a good side Spartak Moscow turned out to be. Celtic manager **Gordon Strachan** talking after the famous Celtic penalty shoot out win against Spartak Moscow in August 2007 at Celtic Park.

61. MARTIN O'NEILL TOLD us that all his family was gathered around the TV to watch the 1967 European Cup Final in Lisbon Cup. Twenty minutes before kick off their TV broke down and everyone was going mad! Luckily it came back on just as the game kicked off. **Stevie Chalmers.**

62. CELTIC LEGEND **BILLY McNEILL** had so much respect for Jimmy McGrory that he always called him Mr. McGrory or Boss, even after Jimmy was no longer the manager.

63. I WAS A dumpling at school. I got out just before the exams, and I started work as a motor mechanic. **Charlie Nicholas**

64. I WON'T BE able to sleep after such an emotional night. I hope the TV is good at four o'clock in the morning. **Gordon Strachan** talking after the Celtic penalty shoot out victory against Spartak Moscow in August 2007 at Celtic Park.

65. "AN OLD HEAD on young shoulders." **Jock Stein** talking about 20 year old George Connelly, who had just scored a wonderful solo goal against Rangers in the 4-0 Scottish Cup final in 1969.

66. BOBBY MURDOCH WAS someone who never forgot his roots. He was proud to be a Celtic fan and a Glasgow guy. **Tommy Burns** talking about the player who was the heart of the Lisbon Lions

67. AFTER A SCOTTISH Cup tie at Celtic Park, **Mark McGhee** had to stop an angry raging Tommy Burns from going for Mick McCarthy in the bath after the game – and Celtic won that game! Disagreements between players who have a passionate sense of pride in playing and winning for Celtic, are not uncommon.

68. SINCE I WAS a kid playing in the streets of Bellshill in my green and white jersey, all I had ever wanted was to play for Celtic. Now I was captain of their European Cup winning team. And being captain at Parkhead means much more than being merely the man who carries the ball out. **Billy McNeill**

69. IN 1977 CELTIC won the **World of Soccer Cup**. This was a four team tournament played in Australia: the teams were Arsenal, Red Star Belgrade, the Australian national team and Celtic. The Hoops beat Red Star 2-0 in the final.

70.   IN JUNE 1968 Celtic beat AC Milan 2-0 in Toronto to win the **Cup of Champions**. Bobby Lennox and Charlie Gallagher scored the goals.

71.   A PAINTING OF the transatlantic liner **R.M.S. Celtic** hangs on display inside Celtic Park. This great ship travelled between Liverpool and New York, stopping off at Cork to pick up Irish emigrants to America. It sank in December 1928 during a storm.

72.   " A BIG thanks to all the Lisbon Lions for all the braggin rights they allowed us to have over the last 40 years." Celtic Supporter in a supporters club in Windsor, Canada.

73.   I SEE CELTIC maybe two or three times a year, but obviously I don't bother watching Rangers. I don't think they play good football anyway, not the type of football I like. It's just hump it all the time which is not my type of game. **Tommy Docherty,** ex Celtic player

74.   I'M CHUFFED TO have scored 273 times in 589 appearances as a winger for the club, especially since I had about 400 good goals wrongly ruled out for offside! **Bobby Lennox.**

75.   FOLLOWING IN THE footsteps of Rolando Ugolini, Paolo di Canio and Enrico Annoni, Massimo Donati became the fourth Italian to play for Celtic when he signed in the summer of 2007.

76.   " THEY WERE just gathering dust." Celtic's **George Connolly,** who sold his medals at auction in 2007. He sold the Scottish Cup winners medal that he won in the 4-0 thrashing of Rangers, in which he scored a great goal, for £1,495.

77.   " WOULD ANY Celtic supporter interested in a forming a Supporters Club, please write to me? All letters will be answered." Celtic supporter **Willie Fanning** wrote a letter to the Daily Record on 05th September 1944 because he was dismayed at the way the Celtic

board was running the club. This was the beginning of the Celtic Supporters Association.

78.   " I was filling a position in mid field as a wee fat Number four." **Kenny Dalglish** describes himself as a teenager at Celtic. He was mentioned as a possible successor to the fabulous Bobby Murdoch.

79.   " A Labour of Love " Celtic manager **Willie Maley** describes his time at Celtic in a speech at the 50 year Jubilee dinner in 1938

80.   " Celtic owes its existence as he never shirked from the day he was appointed President of the first committee till the day of his death to further the project which to him appealed as his life's work." Celtic manager **Willie Maley** talking about **John Glass**

81.   We are trying to create a culture where excuses are not allowed. We get on with the football. New Celtic manager **Tony Mowbray** speaking in July 2009.

82.   On 25 May 1967 it was a Holy Day of Obligation for school kids in Glasgow. Many were supposed to go to mass at 7 pm in the evening, but priests delayed the start so they could watch the European Cup in Lisbon being presented to **Billy McNeill**.

83.   **Shunsuke Nakamura** made his league debut for Celtic against Dundee United at Celtic Park on 06 August 2005. It was estimated that 3 million people in Japan stayed up until the early hours of the morning to watch his debut on TV.

84.   " Come on boys, Let's do a job". **Billy McNeill** to all his team mates on the bus as they arrived at the stadium in Lisbon before the European Cup final.

85.   When Celtic won their 9-in-a-row league championships between 1966-74 they played 306 league games and lost only 26.

Three players played in over 200 games: Billy McNeill (282), Jimmy Johnstone (229), and Bobby Murdoch (210)

86. WHEN THE MEN were away at Seville in 2003 for the UEFA Cup final, many of the wives/girlfriends at home had their friends and families around to have a party and watch the game on TV. Even the family pet dogs were dressed in a Hoops jersey!

87. A SUCCESSFUL CELTIC club are bigger than a successful Manchester United. **Tommy Docherty**

88. I SHARED A room with Tommy Gemmell before the European Cup final in Lisbon. As long as I got him up in the morning, packed his bag for training, kept the room tidy and made sure that he had his Horlicks before going to bed at night, we got on fine. **Jim Craig.**

89. THE WAY HE played against Benfica tells me he has grown from a boy into a man. It was world class and that's the standard he has set himself. People all over Europe will have watched the game and McGeady will be the name on their lips. That kind of display is up there with Ryan Giggs and Cristiano Ronaldo. Few players in the world can produce the skill Aiden showed. Ex Celtic winger **Joe Miller** talking about Aiden McGeady's display against Benfica in November 2007.

90. IN 1902 MANY people were killed in a terracing collapse during the Scotland versus England game at Ibrox. The English and Scottish Football Associations arranged a competition between Rangers, Sunderland, Everton and Celtic to raise money for the victims families. Celtic beat Rangers 3-2 in the final. A few months later to further aid the disaster fund another game took place and this time Celtic beat Rangers 7-2.

91. IN 1945 CELTIC won the Victory in Europe Cup. A competition was held in Glasgow to raise money for charities after the war.

Celtic and Queens Park drew 1-1 in the final, but Celtic won by one corner kick. It was agreed the team with the most corners won the game.

92. One of **Jock Stein**'s favourite saying's to keep Celtic at the top for so long was the need to " **freshen up the team**". Talented young players were given the opportunity to challenge for a first team place.

93. In 1898 the World Cycling Championship was held at Celtic Park. At the turn of the century there was a red cinder track around Celtic Park.

94. Celtic great **Jimmy Delaney** said the Exhibition winning team in 1938 was the greatest Celtic team that he played in. Kennaway, Hogg, Morrison, Geatons, Lyon, Paterson, Delaney, MacDonald, Crum, Divers, Murphy.

95. **John Glass** was a founding member and the First President of Celtic. He came from Donegal and was a joiner in the building trade. His devotion to Celtic helped turn Brother Walfrid's dream into a reality.

96. "Celtic fans are some of the greatest supporters I know." AC Milan's Dutch midfielder, **Clarence Seedorf.**

97. " Look son. If you want to be a footballer make up your mind to be a good one. Always try to play better than you did in your last game. And always put everything you have into it." Lisbon Lion **Steve Chalmers** got this advice from his dad when he was a wee boy.

98. **Jock Stein** won his last piece of silverware as Celtic manager on a tour of Australia in 1977. The 4 team competition involved playing Arsenal, Red Star Belgrade and the Australian national team, the Socceroos. The win was worth $36,000 (£27,720), plus the clubs' guarantees. Celtic went on to beat Red Star in the final at

Olympic Park by two goals to nil, scored by Roddy McDonald and 'Shuggie' Edvaldsson, to win the World of Soccer cup.

99.   " CELTIC IS not just a club, it is a heritage. " Celtic great **Malky MacDonald** who played between 1932 and 1945.

100. "THE TEAM WHO defeats us in a Scottish Cup game will have to do it at the first attempt." **Jock Stein.** Celtic have always had a great Cup winning tradition, and do not get beat often if a game goes to a replay.

101. WHEN I WAS at Newcastle Tommy Craig, who was the Celtic coach in the Centenary winning team, used to say if you're going to do something wrong then do it wrong in a big way. You are better doing that than hiding. If things don't go the way you've planned, you've still got to look for the ball. **Gary Caldwell**

102. I CAN REMEMBER IN the 1980s there was a gate for the unemployed (half price I think) at Celtic Park, and you had to show your broo card (UB 40) to get in. We had a pal who worked in the DSS, so a minibus load of us arrived at the Celtic end with our shiny new UB40s (all of us fully employed). When we got to the gates there was only one queue of thousands of fans at the unemployed turnstile, and every other turnstile was practically empty ! There must have been a helluva lot of Celtic fans working in the DSS. **John, Glasgow**

103. " WE WISH to bear witness to this dignity in defeat which is so rare. The European Cup has become so important that one leaves it usually with bad grace. Certainly when one has won the European Cup and then when one loses in the first round of the following years competition by a doubtful decision by a referee. But Celtic know that it is the game that counts and it is not dramatised. The honour of European football could not be in better hands. French journalist **Jacques Thibert** writing after Celtic had lost to Dynamo Kiev in the first round of the European Cup in 1968.

104. A FEW DAYS after defeating Boavista to reach the UEFA Cup Final in 2003, Celtic played Rangers at Ibrox. Celtic supporters turned up with beach balls, sombreros, sunglasses, and some even braved the cold weather to attend in their swimming trunks! The game had to be delayed to clear the beach balls off the park, which amused the world wide TV audience.

105. "GET THEM TO Celtic Park, make sure they sign a contract and only then show them Barrowfield." Celtic chairman **Brian Quinn's** advice to the new Chief Executive, Peter Lawwell. Celtic's training ground (Barrowfield) was not the best place for attracting new players. Celtic officially moved from Barrowfield and opened the club's new £8 million training complex in Lennoxtown on 10 October 2007.

106. CELTIC CHIEF EXECUTIVE **Peter Lawwell** said: "Naka is a legend and we hope he will play at Celtic for as long as possible. A contract period? It's as long as he wants."

107. THESE BOYS WILL only get that experience through time. You can't give them a tablet. They have to go through tough games with disappointing results like Wednesday at Benfica. Celtic manager **Gordon Strachan** after Celtic lost 1-0 in Lisbon.

108. I LOOK BACK at my time at Celtic with great affection on the 14 years I spent with the club and the wonderful colleagues I had. We were only temporary custodians of Celtic's greatness and I would not change them for anything. **Malcolm MacDonald**

109. "SHOULD PARENTS PREFER, they could send the bread and the children could get a large bowl of broth or soup for a halfpenny, and those who were not able to pay got a substantial meal free. This has been a very great blessing for the poor children." **Brother Walfrid.** He helped establish the "Penny Dinners" for the children in the East End Of Glasgow.

110. "ARE YOU SERIOUS?" Celtic manager **Martin O'Neill's** reply to a journalist at a press conference who asked him a few days before an Old Firm game if it held any significance for his team

111. MANY FOOTBALLERS ARE superstitious and have routines that they must follow on match days. I always had cereal, toast and a banana for my pre match meal. Most of the other players also go for a walk on the morning of the match, but Johan Mjallby and myself will train at half past ten with coach Steve Walford. Celtic skipper **Neil Lennon.**

112. "HE DIDNAE FEED us mince." **Bobby Lennox** talking about Celtic manager Jock Stein. Jock never complicated things for the players, and they trusted him totally when he talked about the opposition players and the system they would play.

113. WE WANT TO show South America as well as Europe that defensive football is finished. **Jock Stein** before Celtic's infamous clash with Racing Club of Argentina in the World Club Championship in 1967.

114. JIMMY JOHNSTONE, was forced to endure a stream of fouls and spittle against Racing Club of Argentina in the World Club Championship. Jinky needed a shower at half-time to wash the spit from his hair, but the water supply had been turned off. Celtic refused to come out for the second half before they'd had a chance to wash, and the interval lasted half an hour while Racing officials searched for the stopcock.

115. JOE MCBRIDE WAS Jock Stein's first major signing for the sum of £22,500. He scored 78 times in his first 77 matches, but then sustained a serious knee injury. He would have broken every goal scoring record that season if he had not been injured.

116. MARTIN O'NEILL WAS asked the day he resigned as Celtic Manager in 2005. " Do you still love this football club? ". He replied,

"Absolutely right, it has been an honour and privilege. I must also thank Brother Walfrid for bringing the club into being."

117. MY JAPANESE FRIEND, Yumie Suga, was speaking to Naka after the game at Celtic Park when he made his debut for Celtic. She loved Celtic, and was telling him the history of the club in Japanese! Singer **Jim Kerr** from the band Simple Minds who is a great Celtic fan

118. " I TRIED to look for **Scott Brown** at the end of the game because I wanted to apologise. I will try to speak with him by telephone, but I also want to take this opportunity to make a public apology". Benfica player Augustin Binya regrets his horror tackle on Scott Brown. Celtic beat Benfica 1-0 in November 2007 at Celtic Park.

119. WE MOVED FROM the heart of the Gorbals , Lawmoor St. to the next neighbourhood , Oatlands , across from Shawfield , around 1950 , just before Castlemilk was populated , where the rest of the Gorbals ended up . My pals and I, around 1952 began going to the games by ourselves. Depending on the weather, we would walk across the Clyde bridge at Shawfield , up through Bridgeton and Dalmarnock to Celtic Park . Otherwise we would get the bus to Glasgow Cross and get the underground train Springfield Rd. Station around the corner from the ground. We used to smuggle our scarves, big woollen things somebody knitted for you, and maybe a rosette that you da had bought you on the way to Hampden for a cup semi , or the Clyde final . We would put our scarves on as we turned up, I can't remember the name of the Street , dead opposite the school at Celtic Park , where the buses used to sit . Everything that you could buy was handmade most probably by the vendors. They used to sell we lead players on a stick pin , you could attach to your scarf , or your jacket .Nae strips in thae days , also popular where the cartoon cards with the players with the big heads on wee bodies , great likeness to the indi-

viduals though . I wish I had those today . Hail,Hail, **John Paton** , So.Florida .C.S.C.

120. I'VE NEVER WENT to a game without wearing something Celtic. I remember as a laddie going to the games with a Celtic scarf with the pinstripes and the tie to match with a tammy that my granny had knitted. Not many supporters actually wore the strip in those days, but plenty of colour was shown. It was the middle 60's before I started wearing the Hoops to the game although I wore them every day. Ma maw putting it through the ringer every night to wash it and have it ready for the next day. Today I still wear a Celtic strip every day especially to a game along with my scarf. It doesn't make me a better supporter, but it sure makes me proud to show people that I support the greatest club in the world. **Joe Clark** in America.

121. I WEAR MY lucky knickers to the games. When I wear them the bhoys always win. Comment from lady at Seville.

122. I WAS A good trainer and put a sweat in. The training programmes that the Celtic coaching staff had in place were really good. Jinky once said that he thought that Big Jock Stein sat up all night thinking up new training routines. His variations were fantastic and there was something different every day. **George Connelly**.

123. WATCHING CELTIC PLAY "live" every week is like watching a new wonderful story. It is better than any Hollywood movie. And the great thing is that the supporters can be part of the performance if they choose. Everybody should cheer their team and shout something positive at least once in a game, no matter how tough it is. **Pub football expert**

124. WE HAD TWO great jokers in the team that won the Empire Exhibition Cup in 1938 – goalkeeper Joe Kennaway and forward Johnny Crum They kept the whole team laughing, and could have been on stage as comedians. But the biggest influence was our

skipper Willie Lyons. He was a wonderful centre half , a great inspiration, and a true gentleman. **Jimmy Delaney**.

125. MY FAVOURITE EXPERIENCE was in Burundi during the Civil War 2007. I was travelling in a military convoy (long story, I have a medical company with offices in Burundi, Rwanda and DR Congo) down the road which runs parallel with Lake Tanganyika. Most of us were nervous due to the very good possibility of being ambushed. All of a sudden I see this young African boy running along the banks of the Lake with a **CELTIC** shirt on !. It was only after about 30 seconds that I realised it **WAS** a Celtic shirt. I sent some of the soldiers to bring him to our vehicle and when they brought him (the poor bugger was frightened out of his wits) I asked him where he got the shirt ? (all in French). His eyes were like saucers when he saw my **Celtic** t–shirt , and he replied " Pappy John, Pappy John." , and he pointed into the bush. We followed his directions for about 3 km's and we then came to a small village and there we met "Pappy John", who turned out to be a red hot Celtic missionary priest from County Clare, and his brother had sent the shirt! We could not believe that a white man was living in an area which was being turned upside down with the Hutu/Tutsi conflict. He was a lovely humble person who just got on with helping the poor. We gave him all of our supplies and I have been back there twice. Unfortunately there was a massacre of Tutsi's by Hutus in Dec 2008 and the village had to be emptied, but I **DO** know that Father John did get back safely to Bujumbura ,the main town of Burundi. I will probably bump into him in some wee village in central Congo some time…..,.now **THIS** is what **Celtic** is all about. **Bill. South Africa**

126. CAN'T GET YOUR kids to eat their greens and vegetables, why not try the **Celtic Soup**? The recipe looks amazingly healthy and is in Mary Contini's cook book called " Dear Francesca". Mary is the grand daughter of Celtic player **Hugh Hilley** who played in the 1920's.

127. "I'VE SEEN HIM on television, and it looked as if the film was speeded up. Johnstone was running like those horses in the old cowboy films. He is fantastic." Arsenal and Northern Ireland full back Sammy Nelson talking about **Jimmy Johnstone**.

128. IN 1988, CELTIC'S Centenary Year, Lisbon Lion **Jim Craig**, who is a great historian of the football club, identified that 275 players had represented Celtic in the hundred year history. The criteria was that a player must have played at least 25 first team games. It is quite a small number of men who have had the honour of representing Celtic.

129. WHEN CELTIC WON the Scottish Cup in 1965 against Dunfermline, Big Billy McNeill was 25 years old – many fans think he was much younger. **Pub football expert**

130. I HAD MY honeymoon at the England v Scotland game at Wembley in 1977. Remember when thousands of people were all on the pitch? Well, we were on the pitch too and I got a bit of turf. It's at our house in Broughty Ferry. **Gordon Strachan** remembers his wedding day on 04th June 1977. Gordon and his bride Lesley joined thousands of jubilant Scotland supporters as they swarmed on to the pitch to celebrate the 2-1 victory. Gordon McQueen and Kenny Dalglish scored the goals.

131. **LOST HUSBAND**: DISAPPEARED 7 days ago just before the European Cup Final in Lisbon. Answers to the name Andy. Last seen wearing a Glasgow Corporation bus driver uniform, a Celtic scarf, and holding his passport. Tell him his dinner is in the bin. Advert in Lost and Found section of the newspaper.

132. I WILL NEVER forget walking out onto the pitch in Seville and seeing a sea of green and white. I scored twice and I felt we had a chance when the game went into extra time. Our fitness was good and I could see us creating chances. Unfortunately Bobo Balde was sent off and with a man down we found it very difficult. At

the end I was very, very, very disappointed. It is still the worst moment in my career, even worse than breaking my leg. I felt terrible, but most of all I felt sorry for the fans. **Henrik Larsson**

133. The first game I can vaguely remember was when I was six years of age. It was the Coronation Cup final. I can't remember much about it, I just remember being there. I can remember coming and standing on the open side of the Celtic End in the rain when they used to carry boxes with that quaint shouting slogan 'get your cold hot pies here!'. **Dr, John Reid**, who was appointed as Celtic chairman in November 2007

134. Celtic played Manchester United at Old Trafford in **Roy Keane's** testimonial game in 2006. Celtic had a ticket allocation of 23,000, which is an incredible amount of tickets for an away game.

136. There is a story about an old man saying that every man and women have three wants in life: the spiritual side has to be looked after, the material side, and the emotional side. His grandfather said, 'My church looks after my spiritual side, the trade union movement and the labour movement looks after the material side, and Celtic Football Club look after my emotional side.'

137. " What good is a million pounds to us if we do not have **Jimmy Johnstone?**" The answer that Celtic chairman Bob Kelly received when he suggested to Jock Stein that Celtic should sell Jinky.

138. The tour of the ground for the pools agents includes a walk down the tunnel, which leads onto the pitch, the path that every Celtic player has walked. It is very easy for us who have done this as players to forget the thrill this is for the people doing it for the first time. Many of the agents have stood in The Jungle supporting the team. Lisbon Lion **Steve Chalmers** who worked with the Celtic Pools when his football days were over. One of the perks of being

an agent was a VIP visit to Celtic Park on a match day and a tour with Stevie. The Celtic tunnel could tell a few tales of the things that happened outwith the view of the fans.

139. "A FEW WEEKS after our heavy defeat in Bratislava I got on a plane in Sweden, and someone walked past me, put his hand on my shoulder and said, "Remember, when you are at Celtic, you never walk alone." Celtic manager **Gordon Strachan** when asked about the negativity directed towards him.

140. I AM NOT a man who is easily scared. But I am not ashamed to admit that I was terrified at that game. I am convinced that Celtic got away with only one serious injury, the attack on Ronnie Simpson, for just one reason, and that was because we lost. **Jock Stein** talking after Celtic lost to Racing Club in the World Club championship game.

141. I WAS BROUGHT up in a Catholic household and if I'd shown any aspect of sectarianism, I'd have been given a boot up the backside by my old man. Celtic legend **Billy McNeill**.

142. IN NOVEMBER 2006 **Shunsuke Nakamura** scored a fantastic free kick against Manchester United in the Champions League. Celtic won 1-0. After the game, rather than celebrating, he went into the gym to go through his full warm down session: running, lots of stretching, a cold bath, and finally a warm bath. Naka was a professional footballer who did everything to take care of his fitness and body.

143. "IT IS A Rutherglen Bhoy who scored the winner in the European Cup Final." My dad shouted at our black and white telly in May 1967. He thought that Bobby Murdoch, from our home town, had scored the winner. **Robert Harvey**.

144. **RAMON VEGA** WAS a Swiss international defender who played for Celtic in the 1990's. The Celtic players used to have a yellow shirt

with the message " I had a Vega" printed on the front, which was awarded to the player with the worst performance in training. Apparently Ramon was not the best in training!

145. HE NEVER COMPLAINED. Teams used to kick him up and down, but he just got on with the game. There have been many whinge-ing players in British football, but I have never seen Naka whinge about anything. Ex Celtic player **Craig Burley** talking about Nakamura

146. THE NIGHT CELTIC beat Shanktar Donetsk 2-1 at Celtic Park with a last minute goal by Donati a Celtic ghirl supporter uttered these words. " Women relate this game to being in labour, a win was born after much agony."

147. WHEN CELTIC PLAYED Boavista in Portugal in 2003 in the semi fi-nal of the UEFA Cup the game was 0-0 on aggregate well into the second half. This suited the Portuguese team , who were happy with a draw and the game being settled by penalty kicks. Every time the ball went out the park there was no ball boys to throw it back on and keep the game going. The Portuguese were trying to kill the game. Then **Henrik Larsson** scored. All of a sudden every time the ball went out of play about 10 ball boys appeared to throw it back on to keep the game going. It didnae work.

148. "LOOK AT HIM. He is as cool as hell." A Glasgow Observer news-paper sports reporter talking about **Jimmy Quinn.** He had just scored his third goal against Rangers in the 1904 Scottish Cup Final at Hampden. Celtic were down 2-0, but Jimmy then scored a hat trick. After he scored the third goal, he just strolled back to the centre spot. This was one of Celtic's early great wins.

149. WHEN I SEE people leaving Celtic Park early I curse their profliga-cy -- what I would do to be there! **Celtic supporter** in America who has to watch the games on TV or via the internet. He is not

lucky enough to be able to go to Celtic Park regularly to watch his heroes.

150. " THEY ARE not very happy." **Tay Baig** was on his stag trip to London with his friends when he ended up in Seville for the UEFA Cup final. He had 1500 guests waiting in Pakistan for his wedding. He phoned home to try and explain why the Cup final had to take precedence over wedding arrangements. His brother said, " His wife to be needs to understand, he's a diehard Celtic man, a season ticket holder"

151. FOOTBALL IS NOT like that. If form was the only factor we would all win the pools every week. **Jock Stein**

152. "I DON'T KNOW how Billy McNeill was able to play tonight. It's a miracle. And Bob Rooney is the man responsible for it. I don't know how Bob did it. Really Billy played that game on one leg. It was a tremendous performance from him. In any other game I would not have risked him." **Jock Stein** praises physio Bob Rooney after Celtic beat Leeds United in the European Cup semi final. Billy had an injured ankle the previous week, but the intensive good treatment by the physio got him fit for the game.

153. A CELTIC SUPPORTER supports his team through good times and the hard times, and is not someone who puts his team down with constant moaning. Celtic Park must never be allowed to turn into a morgue and a place where the moaners and groaners are heard above those who want to support the team. Season ticket holders who complain about stray passes and slag off players from the first minute should go shopping on a Saturday. No sense groaning about the bad pass, if you can't see the good pass. Some supporters seem to get fun putting the boot into a young player who plays his heart out, rather than encouraging the young Hoops man. Remember it is a Grand Old Team to see. **Pub football expert**

154. Soon after the European Cup final in Lisbon, a policeman knocked at a door of a house in Glasgow. The woman of the house opened the door and was astonished to see her son in his Celtic colours being held up by two policemen. " Where the hell have you been?" she shouted. " you are supposed to be on your honeymoon in Blackpool".

155. I don't know their psyche, but what I do know is that they've got top, top players. They've won things – World Cups, European Cups. You just don't switch off when you're built that way, it doesn't happen like that. They are real competitors. **Gordon Strachan** talking about AC Milan before Celtic played them in December 2007.

156. He brings much needed colour to Scottish football with his opinions and sense of humour. I wish there many more like him in our game because it would be a hell of a lot more entertaining. With Gordon Strachan around there is always something to talk about . But it can be painful some time watching him give my colleague Stuart Lovell a hard time during live TV interviews before or after a game. **Scott Booth**, Setanta Sports TV commentator.

157. One thing was drummed into us. You never did anything that brought the club's name into disrepute. **Malcolm McDonald** who played for Celtic between 1932 and 1945.

158. " We knew he was pining for home": Celtic manager Willie Maley after he signed **Tommy McInally** from Third Lanark in 1925. Tommy had been transferred from Celtic in 1922. He was a great character and goal scorer for Celtic.

159. Naka is very very fit. When we do the ProZone, which tells you how many metres you have run in a game, he is always one of the best. He runs over 12 kilometres in a match. **Aiden McGeady** talking about his team mate Shunsuke Nakamura.

160. I'VE ALWAYS KNOWN that Aiden McGeady has that drive and determination to be a top player. I remember sitting in the office with youth team coach Willie McStay at Barrowfield and Aiden thought he should have been in the first team. He was just 15 years old. That is not a bad thing as long as you have something to back it up, and Aiden has. **Tommy Burns**.

161. "I DON'T KNOW if John Valentine (the Rangers centre half) had no faith in George Niven (the Rangers goalkeeper) or Niven had no faith in Valentine, but ultimately they had no faith in themselves, something you can sense very quickly on a football field, and inevitably the game became a rout." **Bobby Collins** of Celtic speaking after beating Rangers 7-1 in the 1957 League Cup final.

162. IF YOU KNOW of any old mine workings we'd be pleased to hear from you. Consultant engineer Brian Veitch asking local Cambuslang residents for feedback when doing the survey for the proposed new Celtic stadium in the Cambuslang area in the 1990's.

163. I HAD AN almost telepathic understanding with Bobby Murdoch in midfield. I swear that in the 1967 European Cup final, even if I had been wearing a blindfold, I would have known where to find Bobby on the Lisbon park. Jock Stein's instructions were always that the ball had to go from the back four to the midfield, Bobby or me. Only in emergencies was the ball to be belted up the park. **Bertie Auld**

164. WHEN JOCK STEIN arrived as manger he taught us that just PLAYING football was not enough. For a club like Celtic success was necessary. **Billy McNeill**

165. " To WIN our next game." This was **Jock Stein's** reply when asked what his ambition was in football.

166. " HAW MCDONALD: the Titanic performed better than you on ice." Fan shouted to Celtic centre half **Roddy McDonald** during a game at Tannadice when the playing surface was frozen

167. CELTIC ARE ALWAYS a credit to football, they play with their hearts. I am happy they have qualified for the last 16 of the Champions League. They deserve it. I wish them luck at the next stage. **Clarence Seedorf**, AC Milan.

168. TOMMY BURNS WAS an out-and-out football man and if there were two boys playing on a park across the road from his house he would run out and watch them playing. That was the kind of guy he was and he just loved the game. Tommy was from the old school of football management and wanted his players to become better players, but also better people. **Malky Mackay**

169. IF HE LOOKED in the mirror the wrong way he'd try and start a fight with his own reflection. He was not frightened of anything. He could fly off the handle at the smallest thing, and would go into a rage if he could not find one of his boots in the dressing room. **Paddy Crerand** talking about a young Bertie Auld.

170. WILLIE WALLACE WAS a hard man. If a defender kicked him, he made sure he kicked him back, and he would fight the battles for wee Jimmy Johnstone and me as well. **Bobby Lennox**

171. WE MUST UNDERSTAND - and understand fully - that we shall get bad breaks in a game many more times in future, but that we must take it in our stride and get on with the job of winning. We must also realise that a likely result of many of the matches we play will be a draw because of the type of game our opponents set out to play. Undoubtedly the answer to the planned, extra defence, is for us to use every football skill and wile that we possess. We only lose our effectiveness if we fall for playing the type of spoiling game the other team wants to impose on us. And there is absolutely no

sense in getting caught in their traps when we know the kind they are. **Jock Stein** after Celtic drew with St.Mirren in 1966.

172. IF WE PLAY to our best form then we will win all right. I know this. But footballers are not like pieces of machinery. We have to beat them as individuals. They are human beings and are not infallible. Celtic chairman **Sir Robert Kelly** before the 1970 European Cup final against Feyenoord.

173. I AM DELIGHTED with the team. Boys like George Connelly, Kenny Dalglish and Lou Macari learned more in one-and-a-half hours than some players learn in one-and-a-half-seasons. **Jock Stein** after Celtic played Uruguayan champions Nacional at Celtic Park in 1971 winning 3-0.

174. " WHEN YOU say " CELTIC" people know who they are and what kind of club it is. Every football person in the world knows Celtic." Dutch striker **Jan Vennegoor of Hesselink** when he signed for Celtic

175. BRENDAN'S (LAVELLE) dedication, passion and knowledge for his club, once caused him to wager his house on what minute Larsson would score. He was within the 2 minute tolerance, and so still has a roof over his head. Brendan is the chairman of the Achill Island CSC. http://come.to/achill-celtic

176. AIDEN MCGEADY HAS always been his own man and a strong-minded wee guy. He had unbelievable confidence in himself and sometimes Aiden could be on the impudent side. It seemed like every other week I'd be giving him the verbals until it finally dawned on him that I wasn't trying to put obstacles in his way. I was actually trying to teach him that humility is an important quality to have as a player. **Tommy Burns**.

177. IF YOU'RE A winger at Celtic then you're instantly compared to Jimmy Johnstone. If you're a striker you're the next Henrik

Larsson. We live with hysteria every day at a club like Celtic. It's happened in this country since football began. I didn't worry it would get out of hand with Aiden McGeady because I knew him too well. This boy knows he's been gifted by God, so he eats properly and he makes sure he rests in the appropriate manner. He knows where he's at in the game and his other piece of good fortune is that Aiden comes from a level-headed family. What's been overlooked is that McGeady's a Celtic guy, and so is his dad, John. The club owes a debt of thanks to him because there was more money on offer for his son to join other clubs when he was one of the most sought-after kids in the country. But Celtic were good to Aiden and his head was never turned. **Tommy Burns**.

178. "THEY WOULD RUIN the most famous jerseys in football." Celtic chairman **Sir Robert Kelly** objected to players having numbers on their jerseys.

179. I DON'T THINK anyone has given more of their life to any club, or done as much for any club as he did for Celtic. **Jock Stein** talking on the death of chairman Sir Robert Kelly.

180. **NEIL McCALLUM** SCORED Celtic's first ever goal in a 5-2 victory over Rangers in May 1888. It was a header from a corner by Mick Dunbar. The second goal was also a header and was scored by James Kelly. The newspaper reported that Celtic played a short passing game and kept the ball low.

181. HIS FAMILY CALLED him Willie, and also his friends at school. I wrote a few lines in my newspaper when I was reporting on a Blantye Vics game he played in when he was farmed out from Celtic, and I called him Billy, and the name stuck. Years later he told me he had to change his signature because of what I had written. I think **Billy McNeill** sounds better than Willie McNeill. Sports journalist Allan Herron.

182. JIMMY JOHNSTONE WAS nominated the third best player in Europe in a French Football poll of sports writers in 1967. He was also selected for the 1967 " Earth team to play for the Universe".

183. IF CELTIC PLAYED on the moon, there would be supporters there to cheer us on. **Jock Stein.**

184. WHEN JOCK STEIN came to Celtic as manager, there was a snooker table that the players used. He got rid of it and brought in a table tennis table. He liked to play with the players. But he used to get annoyed if he got beat, or if someone served to his weak back hand. " That is no right. Serve it again properly" he used to yell at any player brave enough to try it. **Davie Hay**

185. ONE OF THE Celtic's claims to fame was that their floodlight towers were the highest in the world, standing 208 feet above the playing surface. They were first switched on 12th October 1959 for a friendly against English champions Wolves.

186. " THIS TEAM will never be beaten". **Jock Stein** to his friend Bill Shankly on the bus after the victory in Lisbon in 1967. (this was over heard by Bertie Auld)**.**

187. WHEN THINGS ARE tough for Celtic, the players need to have a long hard look in the mirror and ask themselves if they see a winner staring back at them. If not, they should give up their jersey to someone else – something they will regret for the rest of their life. **Pub football expert**.

188. THE NIGHT BEFORE the Lisbon European Cup final I slept well. Ronnie Simpson and I were rooming together as goalkeepers usually do, and we both had a decent kip. But some of the others were hyped up, like Jinky, Bobby Lennox, and Murdy. Me and Ronnie were different, we just relaxed and conked out. **John Fallon**, Celtic substitute goalkeeper at the Lisbon final in 1967.

189. I've beem a Celtic supporter for more than 50 years. I was at the 1953 Coronation Cup final. I'd walk from Carntyne in the east end of Glasgow to Parkhead and back, sometimes in the pouring rain. Big Sam McGuinness, my pal, used to walk with me and he still attends the games. He was my guest for my first Celtic match as chairman. New Celtic chairman **John Reid** in December 2007.

190. "Scottish football has been laughed at long enough. Now maybe they'll take it seriously." **Jock Stein** speaking about the English press after Celtic beat Leeds in the semi final of the European Cup in 1970.

191. "He died leaving Paradise and now he has gone to another Paradise". Priest at the funeral of a great Celtic fan who collapsed and died leaving Celtic Park after a game.

192. The wonderful vocal Celtic support is worth 6 points every season. **Pub football expert.**

193. The highlight for me was about an hour before the game in Seville when we went out for a warm up and the stadium was filling up. Martin O'Neill was just behind me and he was saying this is brilliant and he wished that he was still playing. Then they played the Fields of Athenry and there was almost 40,000 Celtic fans inside the Stadium all singing it and the hairs on the back of my neck were standing up. **Neil Lennon**.

194. "An acre of Performance is worth a whole world of Promise. Don't tell me how hard you've worked for the Celtic cause every Saturday, tell me what you've achieved for the team." **Pub football expert** who says hard working players who run about without contributing are ten a penny and that you can find them down the Glasgow Green park every week. Celtic fans want to see players with great skill and not road runners.

195. Some managers don't like getting close to players, but I like being close to my players. I like laughing with them. So when I have to be harsh with them, they know that it's only for their own good and the team's good. **Gordon Strachan**.

196. I was at the European Cup finals in Lisbon in 1967 and Milan in 1970, but unfortunately I did not enjoy the games due to the drink. The next European Cup final that Celtic reach, then I will be as sober as a judge. **Jim Tait**

197. I have met some of the people who are organising Celts for Change, and they are not a rabble but are die hard Celtic fans. **Billy McNeill**, December 1993

198. The Jungle might be gone but its spirit is alive here in the Bairds Bar in the Gallowgate. **Bertie Auld.**

199. Joe Cullen was one of the first great Celtic goalkeepers. He played for Celtic between 1892 and 1897. A fan gave Joe a gold watch after he played a great game against Sunderland.

200. " Never forget the power of good that football can bring to the life of a Celtic supporter." This was written in a letter of thanks to Lisbon Lion **Jim Craig,** who had visited a sick fan in a hospital in Belfast. The letter was written by the son of a father who had died. But he had had lived much longer than the doctor's expected. In the last few months of his life he told all his visitors that a Celtic player had visited him, and he proudly showed them the photographs wit ha Lisbon Lion.

201. One day we were playing at Stirling Albion. I fell on to the track as I was going for the ball. I looked up at the fans giving me abuse, and I recognised a face. He was someone that I often gave complimentary tickets to the games. He did not get any more after that game. Big **John " Yogi" Hughes**. Yogi scored 189 goals in his Celtic career, including on his debut against Rangers when he was

just seventeen years old. " Feed the Bear" was a common chant at Celtic Park for Yogi.

202. The midfield is the engine room where victories are forged. If you are outnumbered or outfought there nothing can happen up front, as there will be no supply to the strikers, even if you played with five forwards in attack. **Jock Stein**

203. I'm not really one who likes to speak about myself. I suppose what's relevant is that I didn't grow up with a silver spoon. I sold programmes in Tolka Park, which was home to Drumcondra F.C. at the time, and Croke Park at 10 and 11 years of age. I started work when I was eighteen, so as far as my background is concerned I can understand and I can relate to people who have to earn a weekly wage so I don't have to be told what it's like and I haven't forgotten. **Dermott Desmond**.

204. In 35 years involved in football I have never seen or heard anything like it. Paul was booked for bleeding. It is unbelievable. **Gordon Strachan** after Paul Hartley's harsh booking against Hibs at Celtic Park after he was cut.

205. Celtic manager Willie Maley did voluntary work at Stobhill Hospital in Glasgow during World War One (1914-18).

206. In the late 1960's Arsenal manager Bertie Mee wanted to pay a British record transfer fee to bring **Bobby Lennox** to London. But Jock Stein did not want to sell him. A good decision for Celtic.

207. Tommy Burns had a unique personality who made all people feel special. Tommy insisted long-serving Celtic masseur **Jimmy Steel** lead out Celtic at the 1995 Scottish Cup final against Airdrie.

208. I will never forget Henrik's first goal in the game against Porto in Seville. To get such power on the header and get up so high and still head the ball across into the far corner was incredible. I've only managed to watch a video recording of the game once and

I hadn't realised how bad their play-acting had been. Those two things definitely stand out for me. **Neil Lennon** talking about the Seville UEFA Cup Final.

209. **CARL MUGGLETON** WAS a goalkeeper who played for Celtic in season 1993/94. He played 12 games and had 6 consecutive shut outs. When he left Celtic he joined Stoke City.

210. I THINK THAT I am speaking for thousands of Celtic fans in saying that the man to blame for the defeat by Rangers must surely be our manager **Jock Stein**. This was in the letter page of the Celtic View after a 1-0 defeat by Rangers in the New Year's game at Ibrox in 1969. Even the greatest Celtic team manager was criticised for his tactics by a supporter who thought he was speaking on behalf of everyone.

211. "EAT THE RIGHT things. Live the right way, practise, practise, practise." **Tommy Burns** used to say all the time to the young players at Celtic Park

212. JOCK STEIN WOULD have loved Nakamura, because he has the ability to unlock defences, and that is what you need at the top level. **Bertie Auld**

213. FOR A NORMAL 3:00 pm Saturday afternoon kick-off, we leave Portree Square at 7:30 am. Arrival back in Portree can be late, but the craic on the bus usually keeps you going! Waking up and going to bed on a Scottish Island but spending the middle part of the day amongst 60,000 football fans at **Parkhead** is a great way to spend a Saturday. Formed in July 2005 the Isle of Skye Celtic Supporters' Club, members of The Celtic Supporters Association, is now well established with over 80 members. Skye may be a fair distance from **Celtic Park** in Glasgow but a growing number of bhoys make the trip from Skye to see **The Hoops** play their home matches. **www.skyecelticsupporters.com**

214. Belfast Celtic was formed as an imitation of Glasgow Celtic. The teams would play against each other on a regular basis, with Belfast Celtic's ground also called Celtic Park and 'Paradise'. Belfast Celtic presented one of the best away strips ever to be worn by Celtic, a white strip, with a green collar and a green shamrock as the crest. Unfortunately in 1949, they were forced to withdraw from football altogether, due to sectarian elements. They did give Celtic one last gift though, a certain man called **Charlie Tully**.

215. It is thought that the first team to wear the Green and White Hoops were a junior team called St. Anthony's whose home ground is still in Govan next to Ibrox Park.

216. Celtic celebrated 100 years (1903-2003) of wearing the famous Hoops in 2003. Can you remember the first time you wore your Hoops to watch a game? Where was it and what was the score? What did wearing it mean to you ? **Pub football expert**

217. The corner flags at Celtic Park used to have a shamrock on a white background, but these were removed under SFA rules and replaced with the standard ones.

218. Tommy Gemmell enjoyed life to the full and was full of fun. But he never neglected to work on the basics of his game, and was one of the best trainers I've ever come across. Celtic assistant manager **Sean Fallon**

219. **Tommy Gemmell** was the owner of the sportiest car at Celtic Park in the late 1960's. A grey-black Corsair, complete with a " Colonel Bogey" horn!

220. " The 1ˢᵗ thing the Huns seen was Glasgow Celtic". Headline in the Evening Times newspaper. This was the story of **Gabriel Patrick Quinn** who was on the beach in Normandy for D-Day in 1944. He was wearing the Green jersey under his uniform. He

wrote " GLASGOW CELTIC" on the front of the tank that he was in.

221. THE CELTIC CINE Club was formed in 1969 by **John McFadyen**. They filmed in 8mm cine, and the Celtic chairman Sir Robert Kelly donated £100 which helped buy a projector to get the club started. The purpose was to show Celtic on film, and they travelled all around the UK, and even as far as Canada and New York with their film show, which attracted large audiences. They captured the famous 4-2 win over Rangers in 1979 that won the league title for Celtic. This was the night the STV crew went on strike. Luckily there is a film record of this great victory.

222. **TOMMY CALLAGHAN** IS the only player to have been signed TWICE by Jock Stein. What a reference for a players CV.

223. " SCOTLAND HAS made its mark on the world stage in a variety of ways, engineering, economics, medicine, literature and many others. Celtic through their impact on the world sporting scene over the past decade have surely earned a place among those people and institutions whose very name is synonymous with Scotland. " **Frank McElhone,** M.P. and under Secretary of State in the Scottish Office, writing in the souvenir program before a tribute dinner in 1974 organised by the Celtic Supporters Association to honour the players who achieved 9-in-a-row.

224. KENNY DALGLISH HAS been for Liverpool what he has always been, a very good footballer. The only difference now is that he gets more recognition, especially from the crowds at Hampden. When he made a mistake in international games when he was a Celtic player they used to moan, but now they encourage him. **Jock Stein**

225. IN 1971 PARTICK Thistle shocked the football world by defeating Celtic 4-1 in the League Cup Final. Incredibly they led by four goals at the interval! "You know that is the ONLY time I

have ever seen Jock Stein speechless at half-time. His only comments were, 'They've scored four so you can score four." **Tommy Callaghan**.

226. " Bertie of the Celtic." These are the words written on the grave stone of **Bertie Thomson** who played for Celtic 131 times between 1929-1933.

227. It was said that **Jock Stein** could turn an average player into a good player, and a good player into a great player.

228. We were always a team who enjoyed a sing-song and there was no reason that the European Cup final should be any different. In fact for the occasion there was no better chorus than the Celtic song. The tunnel leading to the field in Lisbon acted like an echo chamber and I think the volume of noise panicked the Italians. Maybe that's where the game was won. **Bertie Auld** who started to sing the Celtic Song in the tunnel before the European Cup final in 1967. The rest of the players joined in.

229. On the You Tube website (www.youtube.com) there was a free kick competition filmed between Celtic's Nakamura and the world's greatest player, Ronaldino of Brazil. Naka won.

230. I will not forget the Seville experience to my dying day. When I found out that I was getting a ticket for the Seville final I was euphoric for the next few hours. It was like winning the lottery and even better than a night out with Kylie. **Pub football expert**

231. " The most beloved symbol of the club, the world famous and universally recognised green and white hoops, have been sacrificed at the altar of commercial greed. This abomination is not the jersey worn by Quinn, McGrory, Tully, Johnstone, McNeill, McStay and Larsson."   Celtic supporters everywhere were up in arms over the potential introduction of a new strip in 2001.

232. IN AUGUST 1966 Celtic registered 25 players who could play in the European Cup. Fallon, Kennedy, Martin, Simpson, Craig, Gemmell, Halpin, McCarron, O'Neill, Brogan, Cattanach, Clark, Cushley, McNeill, Murdoch, Auld, Chalmers, Connelly, Gallagher, Hughes, Johnstone, Lennox, McBride, Quinn, Taylor. This included four goalkeepers.

233. IN 1991 CELTIC broke with tradition when **Liam Brady** was appointed as the Celtic manager. He was the first person not to have played with the club who was appointed as the manager. He was only the club's eighth manager in 100 years.

234. PETRUS FERDINANDUS JOHANNES van Hooijdonk, or more commonly known as 'Pierre Van Hooijdonk' has the longest name in the history of Celtic players. It derives from the 17th century, when two farming families in the Enschede area of the Netherlands intermarried. Both the Vennegoor and Hesselink names carried equal social weight, and so – rather than choose between them – they chose to use both. 'Of' in Dutch translates to 'or' in English.

235. CELTIC MIDFIELD STAR **Shunsuke Nakamura** became the first Japanese player to score in the European Champions League when he netted against Manchester United at Old Trafford in 2006.

236. IN THE 1967 European Cup final in Lisbon, Jock Stein asked **Jimmy Johnstone** to keep dribbling with the ball at the start of the game. This was to get the Portuguese crowd to cheer on Celtic. It worked.

237. " A DESERT that will become a Garden of Eden". Secretary **John McLauglin** at the Celtic AGM in 1892 describes the move to the new Celtic Park.

238. IN 1937 CELTIC beat Aberdeen in a Scottish Cup final, watched by a record crowd of 146,433 at Hampden Park. The attendance remains a record for a club match in Europe.

239. THE LARGEST CROWD ever to watch an Old Firm game was 132,870 at the Scottish Cup Final at Hampden in 1969. Celtic won 4-0.

240. THE BRITISH RECORD attendance for a league match is 118,567 on 02 January 1939 at Ibrox against Celtic.

241. ONLY 4 OF the Lisbon Lions were "true" Glaswegians – Simpson, Craig, Auld and Chalmers.

242. JIMMY MCGRORY SCORED 27 goals against Rangers and is Celtic's leading scorer in this fixture.

243. " NEXT TIME I would hope to play with a full deck of cards.' **Gordon Strachan** after a defeat at Ibrox in August 2005. Alan Thompson was sent off after 22 minutes for his first foul of the game by referee Stuart Dougal. Neil Lennon was also red carded in this match.

244. THE ONLY RESULTS I look for on a Saturday are Celtic, Yeovil Town, and Sporting Lisbon. If a team does not wear the Hoops then I am not interested if they win, lose or draw. **Pub football expert**

245. HE DROVE US on to win the league in our Centenary Year. Pat Bonner talking about the magnificent **Paul McStay**

246. I'VE FOLLOWED CELTIC ever since I was a kid, and I always had an idea that it wasn't the establishment club up here if you know what I mean. But the levels people go to get at this club have genuinely surprised me. It's harsh and it is not about football. I have always worked on the principle that if you do not play well then you get stick, but if you do play well, you get praise. That is what being a footballer is all about. But is it not that simple up here. The lengths certain people and certain papers are willing to go to for stories are beyond belief, and I find it very shallow and disappointing. **Craig Bellamy**

247. **MARTIN O'NEILL** ACCEPTED substantial undisclosed libel damages over a Daily Record newspaper allegation that he was joining Liverpool. His solicitor, Paul Hackney, told Mr Justice Eady at London's High Court that the article in The Daily Record, in February 2003, questioned Mr O'Neill's loyalty and commitment to Celtic, and his integrity. The newspaper's solicitor, Patrick Swaffer, confirmed its acceptance that the allegations were without foundation and offered its sincere apologies.

248. "I SEE HIM in the shower and see how he works on his body, and I see his muscles" then obviously thinking that this isn't coming across the right way says: "But I don't look at any other parts of him!". Celtic Dutch striker Jan Vennegoor of Hesselink talking about **Bobo Balde,** who had an amazing physique.

249. IN TEN YEARS my recollection of our manager Jimmy McGrory is that the only time he did not have it stuck in his face was when he was eating. **Charlie Tully** talking about Jimmy McGrory who was always puffing on his pipe.

250. YOU DON'T ACTUALLY realise what you have at Celtic until you leave. I say to everybody my biggest regret was not staying at Celtic. Spanish goalkeeper **Javier Sanchez Broto**, who left Celtic after refusing a new contract.

251. NAKAMURA SIGNED FOR us in July, and made an immediate impact at Celtic, not least because it seemed that every time you opened a cupboard, a Japanese reporter would fall out. **Neil Lennon**. There are a number of Japanese journalists who work full time in Glasgow reporting back to their newspapers in Japan on every game that Naka plays.

252. THE FIELDS OF Athenry was sang for the first time at half time at a game between Celtic and Falkirk in April 1996 at Celtic Park by the writer **Peter St.John**.

253. "MY FATHER TOLD me that if you do not support Celtic, you go to hell." Comedian **Frank Skinner**

254. ALTHOUGH SEASON BOOK sales remain high, attendance at home games has dropped markedly this season. The North Stand Upper has always been cold, leaky and regularly devoid of toilet paper (if visiting from some of the better catered areas of the ground, it is always a good idea to bring your own), but at least we had plenty of company in the past. **www.celticquicknews.co.uk** on 31/12/2007

255. MY FIRST THOUGHT was to ask myself how this awful thing could have happened to someone so young. The lasting tribute to Phil should be his qualities as a Human Being. It is important he should be remembered as a man first of all and a football player second. There are some horrible people in football and sometimes you wonder why the horrible people get so much more out of the game than the good guys. Phil would never say a bad word about anyone. He was a great example of how we should lead our lives. Celtic's **Tommy Burns** after the sudden death of ex Celt **Phil O'Donnell** in December 2007. He was only 35 years old and collapsed and died when playing for Motherwell against Dundee United.

256. " EVERY GREEN seat has a bottom on it and they've made some noise in here tonight." **John Rawling** on Radio 5 describes the "atmosphere" at Celtic Park.

257. JOCK STEIN ONCE joked " that the only thing Celtic hadn't won in 1967 was the Derby horse race, and Bobby Lennox would have won that if he had been eligible". Buzz Bomb Bobby was electric and no defenders could catch him.

258. REMEMBER THIS WAS in the late 50's early 60's when communication was not so easy. A Celtic supporter's father dies, and he has to tell his brother who lives in America the bad news. The problem

is that he can only afford a few words to put on a   TELEGRAM.
This is what he sent: "Celtic 4 Aberdeen 0, Father died." **Des
Garrity**, Vogue Bar, Rutherglen.

259. I HAD MY Alsatian in the back of the car when I went to a game,
a young lad in a Rangers top asked me if he could watch my car,
I replied, I don't need anyone to watch it as the Alsatian is in the
back, the young lad replies, "Mister, can your dug blow up tyres
?". **Des Garrity**

260. " YOU WILL go to the big bad fire!" Celtic's great inside forward
Tommy McInally used to say to others who used bad language.
Although he was the comedian of the team, he disliked swearing.
He scored over 100 goals in his Celtic career.

261. " IF I ever make a coaching video for young children, I would
begin with the footage of Kenny Dalglish celebrating the joy of
scoring a goal." **Billy McNeill.**   Kenny smiled a lot when he
played because he was doing what he knows he does best, playing
football and scoring goals.

262. JOCK STEIN LOVED his players to play like men during the hard
games. He always thought that **Bobby Murdoch** was at his best
during Celtic's toughest games.

263. IN PRAGUE IN the semi final of the European Cup one of our
players took more out of himself than almost any other player I
have even seen. Stevie Chalmers was our lone forward that game.
He was kicked black and blue, but took a lot of the strain off our
defence. I thought the punishment he took in that match had affected his fitness for the rest of the season. But I decided to gamble
on him in the Cup Final in Lisbon, and I almost wept for joy when
he scored the winning goal. **Jock Stein.**

264. THE GREAT WORLDWIDE reputation of the Celtic support has been
built up over many years by several generations of supporters. It

is up to this generation, and the next, to maintain and improve it. **Joe O'Rourke**, General Secretary of the Celtic Supporters' Association, January 2008.

265. CELTS FOR CHANGE created history and were the biggest single and most successful mass movement of fans in the history of Scottish football. **Tommy Sheridan**, MP, and Celtic supporter

266. " WHEN I played for Stenhousemuir, Raith Rovers and Hearts , there was a lot of talk in the dressing room about the " musketeer" spirit of Celtic. That one-for-all, and all-for-one stuff. It was brought home to me in the dressing room after I scored two goals for Celtic in the 1967 Scottish Cup final against Aberdeen. Suddenly I got a thump on the back from Joe McBride – he was injured and missed the final. Joe was entitled to feel down in the dumps, but as with every Celtic player now, the club comes first." **Willie Wallace**

267. I USED TO take Aiden McGeady in the afternoons and sit with him in front of videos for hours on end. When you see ability like that, you have to find a way of getting the best out of it. There has been a lot of straight talking with Aiden, but I'd like to think a lot of decent talking as well. People associate me with screaming and shouting, but it's not been like that. **Gordon Strachan**.

268. WHEN CELTIC WERE first formed in 1888, it was common at the end of the game that the players and officials of both teams would get together for some socialising and a few drinks. Many players would sing their favourite song, tell a joke, or recite a poem. Sandy " The Duke" McMahon, who played in the first Celtic team to win the Scottish Cup in 1892, was a well read man, and he used to recite Shakespeare and do impersonations of the famous actors of the day. Can you imagine a similar scene nowadays after the next Old Firm game? He also scored 171 goals for Celtic in 217 games –a remarkable record.

269. MY UNCLE GOT me a trial for Celtic Boys Club under 12 team. When I arrived there were about sixty other boys before me in the queue giving the manager their favourite position. About fourteen of them said they played inside right (which I also played). I thought I would not get a game so I ended up saying that my favourite position was inside left. **Charlie Nicholas**

270. "GOD CREATED LIQUOR to keep the Irish from conquering the world." Sign in **Celtic** supporters bar in Thailand.

271. CELTIC COMPLETED THE signing of Japan midfielder Koki Mizuno in January 2008. "He is a wide player with pace, a good level of technical ability, and likes a one versus-one situation. He is a good crosser of the ball and that will suit our bigger guys, to see crosses come in from both sides. When he came up to our Lennoxtown training ground on his first day he was as bright as a button, a really lively guy and very different to Nakamura. He was right into the Playstation that all the guys have there.That's not Naka. He's sitting in a rocking chair, slippers on and reading some Japanese philosophy. So Koki has a big personality and that's good for the dressing room". **Tommy Burns** talking about Celtic's new signing from Japan.

272. I OFTEN SAY that long term football domination depends on money. In Glasgow, that means the Celtic business model being better than the Rangers model, and our ownership structure being more stable than theirs. **www.celticquicknews.co.uk**

273. CELTIC's **JIRI JAROSIK** has won the League championship with four different teams in four different countries:– Czech Republic, Russia, England and Scotland.

274. CELTIC FOOTBALL CLUB is more important than sex wee man. Fans can become clinically depressed if Celtic are not scoring every week. **Pub football expert**

275. I signed **Martin Hayes** from Arsenal for £600,000, but within two weeks I regretted it. I knew that I had made a mistake. Martin was a good lad but he was quiet by nature and seemed short of confidence. I think he only played about seven games for us. Celtic manager Billy McNeill

276. Everyone who plays right back for Celtic will be compared to one player and one player only, the great **Daniel Fergus McGrain**. He is a living legend. He was a master of his trade and even today in 2008, he is still always encouraging the young players at Celtic Park. **Pub football expert**

277. Perhaps he was not ruthless enough to be regarded as a really top class football manager. Which is something else he can be proud of. Ex Celt **John Colquhoun** talking about Tommy Burns

278. The Provie Cheque was a life saver. That is how I got to Milan in 1970 for the European Cup Final against Feyenoord. The whole trip including flight and the hotel room cost me 36 pounds on tick. I just told my Dad that I was going to the game, quit my job, and went to watch a bit of Celtic history. **John the painter**

279. In your career there are some games when you can do no wrong and Aiden had one of those days today and he was a joy to watch. It's not just about skill, but also the work he puts into it and the determination. It was one of those games where everything went right for him, and he should get the video so that he can show his grandkids when he's an old man. Gordon Strachan talking about **Aiden McGeady** after Celtic beat Aberdeen 5-1 at Pittodrie in February 2008.

280. When the Queen awarded **Bobby Lennox** the MBE in her New Year Honours List of 1981 the commendation read: " For services to Celtic FC."

281. I JUST WANTED to show him the game isn't easy " **Jock Stein** talking about Vic Davidson. Jock had brought him on as a substitute in the home leg of a European Cup tie. Vic had loads of potential as a young Celtic player, but Stein wanted to show him at that level of football, natural talent wasn't enough, and it had to be supported by application, spirit and a willingness to listen to sound advice from experienced professionals.

282. IT WAS ONE of my greatest moments as a player. **Jock Stein** talking about the day he lifted the Coronation Cup in 1953 when Celtic beat the great Hibs team 2-0 in the final. During the two week competition Celtic played in front of huge crowds at Hampden: 58,000 against Arsenal: 73,000 against Manchester United in the semi final: 117,000 in the final against Hibs.

283. **CHARLIE TULLY** WAS the only Celtic player who called chairman Sir Robert Kelly by the name of " Bob". All the other players had to call him Mr.Kelly

284. CELTIC MANAGER **WILLIE Maley** (1897-1940) won 16 Scottish League titles: 14 Scottish Cups: 14 Glasgow Cups and 19 Glasgow Charity Cups 285.

285. CELTIC MANAGER **JOCK Stein** (1965-78) won 1 European Cup. 11 Scottish League titles.11 Scottish Cups, and 6 Scottish League Cups

286. WHEN CELTIC WON their nine-in-a-row league championships they were known for their fitness. They scored 868 goals during these years, with 467 being scored in the second half of their games. Between the 73rd minute of a game and the 90th minute, Celtic scored an incredible 204 goals.

287. **JOCK STEIN** WAS always available to the press, providing routine news on his team, arguing, trying to influence public opinion, putting Celtic's case forward, and at times winning press friends

by helping them with a story on a dull day. Sports reporter John Rafferty writing about Big Jock

288. **Konrad Kapler** was the first Polish player to play for Celtic. He signed in 1948 and played 8 games. He played outside left.

289. In the Centenary season in 1988 the players were out every weekend at supporter functions and we were treated like Kings and we all loved it. I remember my time a few years later as part of the Celtic management team and trying to get players to go to supporter functions was torture. **Billy Stark**

290. The day after Dixie Deans signed for Celtic we flew out to Malta. I told him that it was a Celtic ritual that new players had to get up and sing a song to the team. He was not the shy type, stood up, took the mike, and belted out " Band of Gold" **Dave Hay.**

291. **Paulo Di Canio** played in a few derby matches with his clubs around the world. He said you can take any derby, double it, and then multiply it, and it will not be the equal of an Old Firm game.

292. When Celtic played Partizan Tirana from Albania, the Celtic captain **Roy Aitken** handed the opposing captain a Celtic pennant. The Tirana captain handed big Roy a book on Albanian architecture!

293. "I scored the winner at the Celtic end and jumped over the advertising boards and was mobbed by my team mates. I had scored the winner and I thought I was cool, but then I ran back onto the pitch and my face was covered in dirt – somebody had rubbed mud on my face." **John Collins** describes scoring the third goal against Cologne in the UEFA Cup. Celtic had been down 2-0 from the first leg, but won 3-0 at Celtic Park.

294. In 1896 Celtic beat Partick Thistle in the semi final of the Glasgow Cup. After the game Thistle lodged a protest that the Celtic team

sheet was not accurate. For example, the tenement number in the home address of a player was wrong. Thistle lost their protest.

295. **BILLY McPHAIL** SCORED a hat trick in the 7-1 win over Rangers in the 1957 League Cup final. He gave his winners medal to Archie McDougall, the Glasgow orthopaedic surgeon who had earlier saved his career. Billy suffered a number of series injuries in his career including two cartilage operations, which were career threatening in the 1950's.

296. I DON'T THINK there is a ground in the world like Celtic Park that inspires a team so much. **George McCluskey** recalls the night in 1980 when Real Madrid froze and the Celts triumphed 2-0. McCluskey and Johnny Doyle were on target as Celtic beat Real in the European Cup quarter-final first leg.

297. THE THING THAT separates players of similar ability is how you handle knocks. Along the way, something will happen. Someone will tell you that you're not good enough or you'll be rejected. Do not let that sidetrack you from achieving your goal. Celtic's **Alan Stubbs** advice to young footballers

298. LET'S SAY THE truly great player has five prime assets. We are probably looking at players here who have three, perhaps even two. We have to try to improve them into a three or a four. Five out of five, you're looking at Henrik Larsson and that class. So we have to settle, as things are, for second, third or even fourth-tier players. What we have to do is maximise the potential of those we have. It's part of the financial level at which we have to operate. Celtic manager **Gordon Strachan** realises Celtic cannot compete with the annual £40 or £50 million received by Manchester United, Arsenal, Chelsea, Barcelona, Milan, Real Madrid etc from contracts with satellite television companies. Celtic get only £2 million annually from domestic television.

299. WHAT OTHERS EXPECT of me is not as important as what I expect from myself. **Henrik Larsson**

300. THAT'S THE BEST squad I've come across in my life in terms of naturally talented players. You might have come up against a more formidable machine in Sir Alex Ferguson's team, which had Keane, Beckham and all of them. But, for natural talent, Barcelona are phenomenal. Celtic manager **Gordon Strachan** after Celtic lost 3-2 to Barcelona at Celtic Park in a European Championship game in February 2008. Barcelona were fantastic that night.

301. PEOPLE MIGHT SAY they are simple passes. But I still say the 10-15 yard pass is the most important in games. Barcelona proved that. If you look at where their moves started, it was always combinations involving 10-15 yard passes. Then, when the time was right, the bigger, killer pass was played. They also have tremendous move-ment. But this comes from their ability to keep the ball so well. This allows the guys up front to get into dangerous positions. If you keep the ball, strikers can, in their own time, walk into where they can hurt you. **Gordon Strachan** after the game with Barcelona.

302. **BERTIE PEACOCK** WAS so thin as a young man that Celtic chair-man Bob Kelly ordered him to drink a bottle of Guinness every lunch time to add on some weight. It worked, and Bertie went on to play over 450 games for Celtic. He was captain of the team that beat Rangers 7-1 in 1957.

303. PLAYERS LIKE YOUNG **Paul McStay** are totally exceptional. He is very mature, calm, sensible, and able to cope with pressure. People kept telling me he was getting tired when he was introduced into the first team, but he turned out to be our best player. We got to a stage where experienced players were looking to him for help instead of the other way round. Manager **Billy McNeill** talking about Paul McStay in 1982.

304. "I LEARNED TO swear – anyway it beats boiler making in the ship yard." Celtic's **Johnny Madden**, who was a boiler maker to trade, when asked if he had picked up the local language in Prague. He left Celtic to join Slavia in Prague. Johnny was a centre forward and had played in the Celtic championship winning teams in 1893 an 1894. He was one of the first Scottish players to play in Europe.

305. " IT'S BEEN a nightmare. The police described it as a freak snow storm. It was unbelievable. You could not see more than 2ft in front of you, and the bus couldn't move." **Ronnie Mitchell**. A total of 82 fans from the Saltmarket Celtic Supporters Club from Glasgow were heading back from Barcelona in March 2008 when they had to abandon their double decker bus in the Pyrenees in France during a blizzard. The fans, some who were only wearing replica shirts and shorts, had to walk more than a mile to a ski chalet, guided by French police, to find safety. It took them 3 days to get back to Glasgow.

306. DAVID MURRAY COULD have offered to pay me a £1million per week and I would still have said NO. Honestly, I'm being serious when I say that. I didn't ask him for time to think about it. That would have been a waste of his time and I didn't want to do that. There was no way that I could ever pull on a Rangers shirt after all that I achieved in five years at Celtic. Ex Celt **John Hartson** reveals that Rangers tried to sign him when he left Celtic.

307. CELTIC PLAYED REAL Madrid in Alfredo Di Stefano's testimonial game in Madrid soon after Celtic had won the European Cup in Lisbon. It was Celtic's last game of the season. Jimmy Johnstone was fantastic and got a standing ovation from the Madrid fans after Celtic's 1-0 victory. The Celtic players stayed in a hotel after the game, and the next morning Jimmy and his wife were going on holiday. He came out the hotel in the morning with their suitcase and shouted for a taxi. " Where too ?" asked the driver. " Benidorm please driver" replied Jinky. He hated flying, but prob-

ably did not appreciate that Benidorm is a few hundred miles from Madrid.

308. JIMMY McGRORY is Celtic's greatest goal scorer. He was known as the " Golden Crust" and scored hundreds of goals with his head. One day when he was manager at Celtic Park he was standing with his bowler hat on, smoking his pipe, and watching the players at a training season practicing crosses from the wing into the centre forward. It was not going well. The players were surprised to see Jimmy run on the park and head the ball. " That is what I mean lads".

309. RANGERS TOOK OFF right back Kirk Broadfoot at half time – " I think their Doctor will have to untangle his legs." A newspaper report following Celtics' 2-1 win over Rangers in April 2008. **Aidan McGeady** ran the Rangers full back ragged in that game. (Rangers played with two right backs – Broadfoot and Whittaker – to try and stop Aidan. It didn't work).

310. "GONNY GIE'S A lift over, Mister?" This was a commonly heard shout outside Celtic Park when wee boys asked men at the turnstile to lift them over so that they could get into the game for free. Most men were willing to lift them over.

311. I REMEMBER BILLY McNeill telling players to take a few days away with their family when they were going through a bad patch. Sometimes you need to allow the player time to clear his head and freshen up. I remember going five games without a goal and everyone I met wanted to speak to me about it; the pressure starts to pile up. I only realised the pressure of being a Celtic striker after I left the club; you are not allowed to go into work and have a bad day. **Frank McGarvey**.

312. I AM PROUD to say that I knew **Jock Stein** as a football manager, as a colleague, and as a friend. He was the greatest manager in British football and men like Jock will live forever in the memory. **Sir Alex Ferguson**

313. HE WAS A good tackler , breaks things up, more of a young Bobby
      Murdoch in the back four. Pat works on the principle the bigger
      they are the harder he hits them. Celtic manager Jock Stein talk-
      ing about **Pat McLuskey**. Pat played for Celtic between 1969 and
      1977.

314. IN THE DRESSING room before the 1975 Scottish Cup final against
      Airdrie, **Billy McNeill** announced that he was retiring at the end
      of the game. The players got him a telly for his retirement pres-
      ent!

315. NOTHING IS IN perspective in this town. People talk without think-
      ing, people talk without watching, people talk without knowl-
      edge. People talk with a bias, some people talk with a bitterness.
      Fortunately I'm not like that, I just get on with reality. **Gordon
      Strachan**.

316. I STILL BEAR the scars on my knee from a tackle by Jack Charlton
      of Leeds United. I was very lucky to escape serious injury. His
      boot should have shattered my knee cap. But instead he came off
      worse because there was flaw in one of his studs, it cracked, and
      went up through his boot and broke his toe. **Bobby Lennox**.

317. **ALLAN MARTIN** WAS centre forward for Celtic in 1895-96, and he
      was the top goal scorer that season. He was a part time player: he
      worked as a furnace man in the iron works and when his shift was
      finished he played for Celtic.

318. **SAMMY WILSON** IS a famous player in the Celtic history. He was
      a part time player and signed on free transfer from St.Mirren in
      1957. He scored the first goal in 7-1 League Cup final victory over
      Rangers. He was back at his work the next day in the garage to
      make up time lost for playing football.

319. IT WAS HIS passion and love for his family and for life itself that
      made Tommy Burns so inspiring. Prime Minister Gordon Brown

talking after the death of Celtic legend **Tommy Burns** in May 2008.

320. TOMMY, I HAVE so many memories: When I was at Charlotte Street school and you and Davie Provan used to pass by - always prepared to talk to us over-excited 12 year olds! Your entire playing career at Celtic. The best football I have ever seen, during the 96/97 season. The Celtic Supporters Rally in April 1997 when, the day before Fergus sacked you (which you would already have known about), you stood on stage and sang "The Greatest Love of All". Tommy, you broke my heart that day and you have done so again. I have never known a man with such dignity and decency. You were and always will be a legend as a player but, most importantly, as a human being. I know God will look after you now.... **Liz & Tim Robinson. This was posted on a local radio website the day Tommy Burns died.**

321. HE HAS A left foot that makes the ball talk. **Jock Stein** talking about Tommy Burns.

322. THE QUALITY OF your life can't be quantified in pounds and pence. **Tommy Burns**

323. I TOLD THEM they had a basic choice. They could either accept second best, in which case they were not good enough for Celtic, and not good enough for me: or they were going to try harder to be first. I also changed the training set up from physically demanding work to a quicker pattern. Celtic manager **Billy McNeill** to his players after a defeat by Aberdeen. It worked. Celtic went onto win the league.

324. HE IS A right moody bastard in training and on the pitch. That's what gives him his edge. He maybe does not have the electric pace that separates the real top-class players, but he has more than made up for that. The first thing that struck me about him was his size. It doesn't look like it, but he has a massive build and really

big shoulders. It gives him his strength and power. Ex Dundee United manager Ian McCall talking about Celtic's **Barry Robson**. McCall had signed Robson from Inverness Caledonian Thistle for £50,000 when he was manager at Dundee United.

325. " A GREAT player, who came to the game as a boy and left it still a boy: he had no predecessor, no successor. He was unique". Sports commentator John Arlott talking about Celtic goalkeeper **John Thomson** who died at 22 years old

326. THERE WILL BE times when you're on top and you've got to enjoy them when they arrive. But you need to be gracious as well. Because there will also be times when you're not on top and it's about how you handle them. I would never criticise anyone or gloat. Celtic skipper **Stephen McManus** after Celtic won the League in May 2008.

327. " SURELY THERE are enough Celtic songs without introducing religion or politics or anything else?" **Jock Stein**. During a 1972 league game against Stirling Albion he jumped into the Celtic crowd to shout at individuals singing sectarian songs.

328. HE ALWAYS CELEBRATES a Celtic league championship or cup win by getting a tattoo in a strange place. I think he goes to that wee place up the Gallowgate. His wife is going to be really surprised the next time he steps out the shower. **Pub football expert**

329. THIS IS THE club for me. This is where I made myself as a player. This is where everybody got to know me. This is the club I am going to be eternally grateful for giving me an opportunity, when other clubs did not believe in me. **Henrik Larsson**.

330. YOU ALWAYS HAVE talkers in the dressing room and people who are a little bit more calm. He was a little bit more calm, but he was a great guy. Henrik Larsson talking about **Phil O'Donnell**.

331. THE TEAM TALKS by Mr. Stein are a soccer education, and I've never heard anything like them before. I walked out ten feet tall. **Dixie Deans** before Celtic played Hibs in the Scottish Cup Final. Celtic won 6-1.

332. " YOU DON'T play with Jimmy Delaney. You just play to him." Celtic great Malky MacDonald talking about his team mate **Jimmy Delaney**. He was loved by Celtic supporter because of his style of play on the wing. It was said that if the opposition stopped Jimmy, they stopped Celtic. He left Celtic for Manchester United in 1945 because Celtic would not give him a two pounds rise in wages.

333. WHEN CELTIC SIGNED **Jock Stein** from Welsh team Llanelli in 1951, he was offered twelve pounds a week, plus two pounds bonus for a win, and one pound from a draw. Jock was happy to come back to Scotland. He had been in Wales for a season after answering an advert for players: " WANTED: players of proven ability. Transfer fee no detriment"

334. WHEN MY MOTHER sends me the papers from Scotland, big Jock is on the front page and the Prime Minister Harold Wilson is on the back ! Manchester United manager **Tommy Docherty**. Jock was the best known man in Scotland.

335. IT WILL BE important to be well prepared for the match and that we are relaxed. I like to sing before games, sometimes. Celtic goalkeeper **Artur Boruc.**

336. **BOBBY LENNOX** PLAYED at the top level for a long long time because he took care to prolong his career. Every night before a match he went to bed at eight o'clock. The next morning he would take his dog for a walk along the beach near his home. This was a regular pre match routine.

337. **TOMMY " CHING" Morrison** was the first native Irishman to play for Celtic. He was bought from Glentoran in 1895 and played at Celtic for two years. He played in the "Championship of the World" game in April 1896 at Celtic Park, when Celtic beat Aston Villa 3-1.

338. CELTIC IS FAR more than a football club. The traditions, the history, the warmth - you have to experience it every day to really understand this. **Jan Vennegoor of Hesselink**.

339. MARTIN HATED YOU getting booked or sent off for silly things. If you did he went through you like a hot knife through butter. **Neil Lennon** talking about manager Martin O'Neill who helped him focus his aggression in his early days as a young footballer.

340. I EXPECT TO score today. **Pierre Van Hooijdonk** used to tell his team mates before a game. He was a very confident player.In total he scored 57 goals for Celtic in 68 appearances.

341. " HAMPDEN IN the Sun ,we've done it again." Celtic captain **Roy Aitken** to TV reporter Jim White on the field at Hampden after Celtic beat Rangers 1-0 (Joe Miller scored) in the Scottish Cup final. (White was known to be a Rangers supporter).

342. " HOW DO you manage to run so much in this heat?" Celtic's Swedish goalkeeper Magnus Hedman asked his colleague **Henrik Larsson** during Euro 2004: his response was astounding.. " Magnus, the hotter it is the more I run and the more I run the better I feel. "

343. ONE OF THE best Celtic games I have ever seen was the 3-3 draw against West Ham in Bobby Moore's testimonial game in London in 1970. Celtic were dazzling that night and the gasps and comments from the crowd about our performance remain indelibly in my mind. Celtic chairman **Brian Quinn**

344. I HAVE PLAYED at Celtic Park twice and I have never experienced anything else like it. It is the only stadium in the world that I have played in where I could not hear myself think because the noise of the fans was so loud. **Razvan Rat,** left back of Russian club Shaktar Donetsk

345. "I WILL LET you in if you promise not to hit me." **Jimmy Johnstone** to Jock Stein after Jinky had been substituted in a game, threw his jersey into the dugout, and ran up the tunnel into the dressing room. Jock was angry, but could be heard laughing after Jinky shouted though the door to him.

346. " DELANEY IN the centre, the ball was in the net, and there was Jerry Dawson (Rangers goalkeeper), alying in the wet". Song from the 1940's

347. THE 1953 CORONATION Cup competition involved four clubs from Scotland and four from England and was held to commemorate the coronation of Queen Elizabeth. The invited teams were Hibs, Aberdeen, Celtic and Rangers from Scotland, together with Arsenal, Manchester United, Newcastle and Tottenham from England. Celtic beat Hibs 2-0 in the final. (goals by Mochan and Walsh). Celtic great Bobby Evans won the Player of the Tournament award.

348. I HAD MY last nine months as a pro under Gordon and I am just happy that I didn't have to endure one of his pre-seasons, which are quite legendary. Southampton legend Matt Le Tissier talking about his ex manager, **Gordon Strachan**

349. AFTER THE EUROPEAN Cup final in Lisbon, a lone Celtic supporter bedecked in his colours is hitch-hiking just outside Lisbon. A car stops with room for one more passenger. He looks in. " Where are you going tae?" he asks. " Edinburgh" is the reply. " Nae good to me mate, I'm fae Coatbrig", and continues walking

350. WE THOUGHT BARROWFIELD was fine for our training because it was what we were used to. If we'd had a few bad results, Big Jock Stein would make us walk there from Parkhead. But if we had done well he'd let us take our cars and towels so that we could get dried off before heading back. **Bobby Lennox** talking about Barrowfield along the London Road where the Lisbon Lions used to train.

351. IF ANYONE CAN, He can. TV commentator talking about Celtic's Japanese star **Shunsuke Nakamura** as he ran up to take a last minute free kick against Kilmarnock in April 2007. Naka scored, Celtic won 2-1, and won the League Championship. It was an amazing end to the season.

352. YOU ASK ANY player at Celtic and they will tell you the same thing. They want to win. So does the boss, Gordon Strachan. We set out to win every game that we play in. young **Paul Caddis** after Celtic lost 3-1 to Fulham in a pre season friendly in London in July 2008.

353. IT IS NOT his creed or his nationality that counts, it's the man himself. **Willie Maley**

354. I SCORED 109 goals for the club and my old granny could have scored about 60 of them. I got more than my share of tap-ins just because of the number of chances Celtic create. **John Hartson**

355. YOU LIVE AND die by results. You can't simply cross your fingers and hope that your luck is going to change. **Tommy Burns**

356. MY DAD WAS a great player but because of the political situation in Bulgaria, he did not have the opportunities that I've had. I know how lucky I am to play with Celtic. **Stan Petrov**

357. THERE'S ONLY TWO clubs on this planet I wouldn't play for, even for £1 million a week. That's Rangers and Cardiff. **John Hartson**. Welshman John is a huge Swanse City fan.

358. " Shunsuke Nakamura has a hernia problem. He'll go to Germany to see the guy who operated on Darren O'Dea. Naka has an incredible body. There has been wear and tear but this is his body giving him a wee nudge to say, ' Time for a wee rest '. We'll give him a couple of weeks' rest but it's not like he's doing nothing. He's been running in straight lines. His fitness level should be fine because if you stop training for two and a half weeks your fitness level doesn't drop. It usually starts to go after three weeks." **Gordon Strachan**

359. When I first joined Celtic, Davie Provan and Roy Aitken were on £150 a week. Provan was always asking me what I was on and one night we went for a few pints and he got it out of me. He bought the pints to get the information. **Frank McGarvey**.

360. " The Best Footballer Ever seen in Australia." Quote about **Danny McGrain**, Celtic's world class full back. Danny had the fitness and skill to play up the whole side of the park on his own – there was no need for a winger. He was also a ferocious tackler who terrified the best wingers he played against. A truly great Celt.

361. The golf tournament was a great success. Every team of 3 people was joined by a Celtic player and I had the honour of playing with **Henrik Larsson**. Facing a particularly dangerous approach shot over water on a par 5, Henrik meant to play safe but completely mis-hit the ball, sailed over the water and landed on the green! He dropped his club and started laughing like buggery, "It doesn't matter whether it is football, golf or life in general, take all the luck you can get!" **John Howley**, Celtic supporters club President in Orlando. Florida. http://www.orlandocsc.com/tim. htm

362. " The Lisbon Lions had 2 world class players in Jimmy Johnstone and Bobby Murdoch " **Sir Alex Ferguson**

363. BEFORE THE WAR our bonus was normally £2 to win a game, but when we played Rangers we were on a ten pounds bonus to win. Ex Celt **Matt Lynch.** He played for Celtic from 1935 to 1948.

364. I HAVE TO convince the coach that I deserve to be in the team, and that can be difficult. It is not like athletics where you are either slower or faster than someone else. In football someone likes you or they do not like you. It's just a decision. **Andrea Hinkel**, Celtic's German international full back.

365. IN THE NICEST possible sense, I don't think the city of Seville has the faintest idea what is about to hit it. Celtic manager **Martin O'Neill** after Celtic qualified for the UEFA Cup final

366. LOOK AT WHEN we played Barcelona last season in the Champions League. The number of passes we get played against us in a Scottish League game is usually a maximum of 250. But Barcelona completed 700 passes against us! Tell me, how do you squeeze that many passes into a 90 minute game of football? If you give the ball away, it takes a long time and a lot of energy to get it back. **Gordon Strachan**.

367. NAKA DOESN'T DRINK alcohol, so when he wins the Man of the Match bottles of champagne, he gives them to me. I go home and drink and shout " I'm the Man of the Match !". **Daisuke Nakajima**, a Japanese journalist who lives in Glagow and reports all of Celtic star Nakamura's games back to Japan.

368. I HAVE WATCHED him closely since I got here and he is an exceptional talent. I've never seen quicker feet in a footballer than Aidan McGeady possesses. I've got to let such players express themselves on a football field and structure my team around that type of quality and imagination and ability. You build your team around that quality and let it flow, let it go and create chances for you. New Celtic manager **Tony Mowbray** talking about Aidan McGeady

369. My cousin Charles Boyce, who sadly passed away in November, was a fanatical Celtic fan. I now attend the games with his daughter and I sit in his seat, which seems to me to be a large part of what goes on at Celtic Park, The grandpas, dads, uncles who 'attend' the game in spirit, and their names are still on the season tickets I love that idea. **Paul McCormick**

370. "When we opened the new Celtic Park, it was a sign that our club was back, strong and proud once again. I could imagine the pride that the first Celtic committee men and directors in 1888 must have felt. All the fathers and mothers, uncles and aunts, all the grannies and grandfathers, that brought all of us to see The Celtic ". **Tom Grant**, ex Celtic director in the 1990's.

371. Many supporters think **Jimmy Johnstone's** greatest game for Celtic was at Celtic Park in December 1969 when they beat Dundee United 7-2. During the game he went on a mazy run beating several opponents, but he over ran the ball over the bye line, swerved behind the goals, beating two ball boys on the way, came out the other side of the goal, and flicked the ball up into the United goalkeepers hands!.

372. " Mr.Strachan shouts at Naka at half time if he is not playing well." **Makoto Kaneko**, Japanese translator for Shunsuke Nakamura. He sits behind the Celtic dugout at home games, and also sits in the dressing room to translate instructions from the Celtic Management team to Naka.

373. On Wednesday 10th April 1974 Celtic played Atletico Madrid at Celtic Park in the first leg of the semi final of the European Cup. The game ended 0-0. Atletico were probably the dirtiest team to ever play at Celtic Park. They assaulted Jimmy Johnstone at every opportunity, including going up the tunnel. The referee was a helpless Turkish gentleman by the name of Dogan Babacan, but he could not control the game, even although he booked the

first Atletico player after just 7 minutes. The next morning a picture appeared on the back pages of the papers showing the bruising to Jimmy Johnstone. The Celtic team on that dreadful night was: Connaghan, Hay, Brogan; Murray, McNeill, McCluskey; Johnstone, Hood, Deans, Callaghan, Dalglish.

374. THERE WAS A chance when Georgious Samaras went round the keeper and might have shot. People say we were unlucky, but I am not so sure. It is unlucky if you shoot and a dog runs across the goal and blocks it. That's unlucky. **Gordon Strachan** talking aftre the Champions legaue game agains Aalborg of Denmark at Celtic Park. The game finished a 0-0 draw.

375. A CELTIC SUPPORTING policeman left Ibrox in the police bus after a game that Celtic had won. He knew he would have to refrain from celebrating as all his colleagues were Rangers supporters. Their bus drew up beside a Celtic supporters bus at the traffic lights. The fans were chanting, " One John Hartson, there's only one John Hartson". The Celtic supporting policeman smiled and punched the air silently. The Supporters bus then began singing: " One Fenian polis, there's is only one Fenian polis"

376. LISBON LION **BOBBY Lennox** was doing a talk at a supporters club. He was talking about how sophisticated the modern equipment is now in the players training room. He said the players eat far more healthier diets now that in his days, and machines tell the players what to eat and drink the night before a game. " We had one too" he told the audience, " it was called a Jock Stein ".

377. I WAS IN the Air Force stationed in Wiltshire during World War Two and looked after the football and boxing teams. I used to pester the doctor for his sun ray lamp to treat injuries and he got fed up with me. One day he told me to take a course in massage. I got my certificate and it all started from then. I used to help Freddie Mills, the world champion boxer, and he wanted me to travel the

world when he was fighting. But I didn't take up this offer. I was friendy with Jimmy McStay, the Celtic manager, and he asked me to help them out at Celtic Park. **Jimmy Steel**, the famous Celtic masseur. Jimmy was once offered the opportunity to move full time to Manchester United, but did not go. He was only interested in Celtic. He was never paid a penny in all his years by Celtic at his own request.

378. I USED TO sit beside big Jock Stein in the dugout during the games, and he concentrates so much on the game, and can explode at any time. It is better for the rest of us to sit quietly. If you had something to say make sure it is intelligent or keep your mouth shut. **Jimmy Steel**.

379. " KEEP THE head up Paul". **Paul McStay** remembers that Jimmy Johnstone used to come to Celtic Park and always had a word of encouragement for Paul when he was going through a hard time as captain of Celtic.

380. **BOBBY LENNOX** HAD extraordinary speed and anticipation and his sharpness was often too much for some referees and linesmen. " I remember scoring 4 goals against Dundee United at Tannadice, yet we only won 1-0! But the one that rankels the most was when I scored againt Liverpool at Anfield in 1966 in the semi final of the European Cup Winners Cup. We were leading 1-0 from the first game at Celtic Park. I scored in Liverpool but the referee chopped it off, but it was a definite fair goal, no doubts about it. Liverpool beat us 2-1 on aggregate. But later even the ref admitted he called it wrong".

381. CELTIC SIGNED SWEDISH goalkeeper **Julius Hyulian** in 1926 (a year before they signed John Thomson), but there was problems with his travel documents and he had to leave without playing a game. He also did not like the Glasgow weather!.

382. JOCK STEIN WAS a hard man. His code of discipline at Celtic ran your life. I remember him grabbing bottles of bedtime milk from Davie Hay and George Connelly and pouring them down the sink, because they were not part of the preparation for the next days game. Lessons had to be learned early. He was right, and his rules and disciplines were crucial to the careers of many playesr. But Jock had another vital skill. He turned good players into great players with one simple rule: ignore the weaknesses and exploit the strengths. The best example is Billy McNeill, who became the best header of a ball there has ever been. **Lou Macari**.

383. I STARTED OUT as a youngster at Bristol Rovers playing at right back. But by the age of 20 I decided to change to a different position and worked on goalkeeping. I am glad I did. If I had not taken up goalkeeping I think I would still be sitting behind a desk now. **Jonathan Gould**

384. **BOBBY MURDOCH** WAS known as **Chopper** to his team mates. He looked after Jimmy Johnstone on the park if defenders were give Jinky a hard time.

385. " IT IS an honour and a privilege to wear those green and white jerseys. Those people out there (all the supporters) have given a lot to see you wearing those stripes (Celtic did not wear the Hoops until 1903). What are you going to give back to them? ". Celtic's first manager **Willie Maley.** He was in charge of the team for 42 seasons and it is estimated he managed Celtic for over 1,800 matches.

386. **JOHNNY CAMPBELL** ONCE scored 12 goals in a reserve game. He is the only Celtic player to have scored so many goals in one game. He had a good career. He played in the first Celtic team to win the Scottish Cup in 1892. He also played in a game in Pailsey and knocked out three teeth of an opposing fans mouth. The police brough the casualty into the dressing room where he wrongly

identified another Celtic player (Jerry Reynolds) as being the guilty party. In the six years he played with Celtic Johnny Campbell scored 109 goals.

387. THE SLOVAKIAN MAGICIAN **Lubo Moravcik** was playing for German club MSV Duisburg, and was about to move to Japan, when Celtic stepped in to sign him. Lubo is regarded as one of the best two footed players ever to play for Celtic. He knew when to beat a man, when to pass, when to shoot, when to trap the ball with his arse (which he once did against Hearts), and scored spectacular free kicks. He gave many memorable moments to Celtic supporters.

388. JIMMY JOHNSTONE'S FOOTBALL academy was the streets and parks of North Lanarkshire.The boy who grew up to be Jinky played football for five or six hours a day. Before, during and after school. Even when Jimmy was dragged in off the streets, he would continue his practice in the family living room. The endless practice, those millions and millions of touches on the ball, allied to innate skill, made Johnstone unstoppable. Where will the players of the future develop their touch? **Writer Tom Shields**

389. CELTIC PLAYER **STILIYAN (Stan) Petrov** almost became a millionaire soon after he joined Celtic. He won the UK national lottery along with a friend. They predicted five numbers and won £2,000 between them. If it had been the six numbers, they would have won a million pounds.

390. TEN DAYS BEFORE Celtic played Inter Milan in the European Cup Final in Lisbon, they beat Kilmarnock 2-0 in a league game at Rugby Park. The league was already won, and Jock Stein played centre half **Billy McNeill** at inside right to confuse the spies from Milan.

391. NAKA'S QUALITY RUBS off on players around him. He has tremendous vision and he gets people off their seats. The Celtic fans have

always loved entertainers. All the way back to the days of Bobby Collins, Charlie Tully and Kenny Dalglish, Celtic have always had players who could do something a bit different. Jock Stein would have loved Naka. Lisbon Lion **Bertie Auld** talking about Shunsuke Nakamura.

392. " IT WAS a sensational goal, one of the top five free kicks ever scored, if not the best," former England internationalist Matthew Le Tissier, and now a Sky Sports football analyst, talking about Nakamura's free kick against Manchester United at Celtic Park. " It was perfect in terms of technique. We speak about the 'postage stamp'. **Nakamura** hits that spot at pace and when you do that it's impossible to stop."

393. SCOTLAND IS NO longer associated with haggis, bagpipes, Rabbie Burns and the River Clyde alone. It is associated with Celtic and successful attacking football: attacking football the likes of which the European countries, including England, have never seen before. Sport writer **Allan Herron** writing in the Sunday Mail in 1970.

394. ON THE MORNING of the Scottish Cup final against Rangers in 1969 Jock Stein noted that most of the papers tipped Rangers to win. Jock read out a series of the comments that belittled Celtic to the players. We were fuming and ready for the battle ahead. At half time we were three goals up. Eventually we won 4-0. **Jim Craig**.

395. HE WAS THE kind of player who epitomised what every manager looks for in a professional footballer. Jock Stein talking about **Bobby Lennox**.

396. THE FIRST CELTIC Supporters Association rally was held in December 1951 in the St.Andrew's Halls. Among the entertainment that night was Buddy Norton, the Maestro of the Accordian, and Davie Aitken, the Singing Vagabond

397. When I had my year out of football, in season 2004-05, I was on holiday in West Palm Beach, and I was out cycling one day and ended up in some Mexican/Colombian area where I stopped and watched some football. I was the only white person there. People were saying, 'Who's the guy with the wee white legs?'. I love watching football. I'll watch it anywhere. I'd love to stop and watch kids' games here in Scotland, but it would be about five minutes before I'd be abused, so I don't do it here." **Gordon Strachan**

398. I have a dream – it is 10-in-a-row. It is not going to happen if we get on the managers back every time we lose a goal. Our support is more important in bad times that in good. Gonna gie wee Strachan a break lads. **Pub football expert**

399. " Two more laps gentlemen. " Celtic trainer **Alex Bowden** in the early 1960s used to stand in the tunnel at Celtic Park and shout to the players. At that time there was poor lighting around the park, so by the time the players sprinted behind the goals, and down the far side of the park, he could not see them. Some of the players took a wee rest. At that time Celtic did not train with a ball. " You will get enough of that on a Saturday" was the training view.

400. When **Stan Petrov** was a young player in Bulgaria one of his coaches told him that an average player has two or three really good games in a row. A good player has four or five. A really good player has six or seven. And an excellent player has nine or ten good games in a row. Stan said that when he first played for Celtic his performances were average. But when Kenny Dalglish became care taker manager after John Barnes resigned, Kenny spoke to Stan and filled him with confidence. His performances then became much better.

401. " YOU WERE my legs tonight. It is no use me making those passes if no one goes for them. " **Bertie Auld** to team mate Bobby Lennox in the dressing room after Bertie played a great game against Fiorentina. Bertie was widely praised, but he appreciated the help he got from his team mate.

402. IN CELTIC'S CENTENARY Year in 1988, they had the best defensive record of any British team that season. They conceded 23 goals in 44 games.

403. I NEVER WATCH football. When I switch on the telly it is usually to watch golf. I am not really a football fan to be honest. When I was young in Edinburgh I only went to football if my uncle, Eamonn Bannon, who played for Dundee United and Hearts, was playing. **Paul Telfer** who signed for Celtic from Southampton in 2005.

404. DO YOU KNOW that famous Hollywood Boulevard where at the great actors have their hand prints preserved in cement on the pavement? Well, I think on the road up to the main entrance at Parkhead every Celtic player who has scored against Rangers should have their foot print in cement in recognition of their great feat. **Pub expert.**

405. I WOULD RATHER play Gaelic football matches at Celtic Park instead, in order to keep the flag flying above Celtic Park. **Sir Bob Kelly** the Celtic chairman in 1952 when the SFA tried to force Celtic to stop flying the Irish flag.

406. I USED TO walk in Glasgow with my European Cup winners medal round my neck and it made me proud if a Rangers supporter stopped me and asked to have a look at it. **Bertie Auld.**

407. CURLY WATTS WAS the star of the British weekly TV soap program " Coronation Street". He was also a big Celtic fan. The London Celtic supporters Club gave him their T-shirt and he promised to wear it when he went into the Rovers Return pub, which was

a famous pub in the program. A few weeks later the bold Curly walked into to the Rovers wearing his Celtic t-shirt, and it was screened across all the UK.

408. IT IS EMBARRASSING for me to remember posing with him at Parkhead for the press photographers. How do I feel about Maurice Johnstone now ? Well I can't forgive him and I don't think Celtic fans ever will. He disrespected all of us. **Billy McNeill**

409. TREAT EVERY GOAL the same, even if it hits your backside and goes in. Every goal is a good goal. Celtic's **Malky McDonald** to a young Joe McBride.

410. IF A SPECTATOR caused any trouble during a game then he could expect Celtic manager Willie Maley to come into the crowd and sort him out. **Dr.Thomas McKail** speaking in 1997. He was a 100 years old and he was thought to be the oldest living Celtic supporter. He attended his first game with hid dad in 1906.

411. **JOE CASSIDY** WAS described as the smallest and cleverest thing to ever appear in a Celtic jersey when he made his debut aged 16 in 1912. He scored 104 goals in his Celtic career. Jimmy McGrory said he learned the art of heading a ball from Joe.

412. **KENNY DALGLISH** WAS the first professional footballer to be awarded with the freedom of the City of Glasgow.

413. MY FATHER WAS killed in a railway accident when I was 10 years old and my mother was expecting my younger sister. I had a background where I knew how difficult it was in life. Back then, it was hard. But we were always fed well, clothed well, and we came from a mining village (Chapelhall) where people shared with each other. Lisbon Lion **John Clark**

414. WHEN YOU TAKE on most sides you think you can beat them in a square go, but Manchester United are different. There's nothing new you can do to stop them playing. Unless I go back to Jim

Leishman's 5-5-0 formation when he came here as manager with Dunfermline once. That was absolutely fantastic. No strikers. Jim said he just stumbled across that one. **Gordon Strachan** after Celtic lost 3-0 to Manchester United.

415. JOHNNY DOYLE WAS the only player I knew who would turn up for matches wearing a Celtic scarf with his suit. **Frank McGarvey**

416. CELTIC PLAYED IN their first Scottish Cup Final on 02 February 1889. They lost 3-0 to Third Lanark Volunteers. The game was played at Hampden and the there was a snow storm just before kick off. The players from both sides threw snow balls at each other as they ran out before the game.

417. **GLEN DALY** RECORDED the classic 'The Celtic Song" in 1961. It was written by Liam Mallory and released on the Piccadilly record label.

418. YOU CAN ALWAYS tell a Celtic house in Glasgow by the wee statue of **Glen Daly** on the mantlepiece. Andy Cameron, Glasgow comedian and a well known Rangers fan.

419. LUBO MORAVCIK WAS a wonderful player who hated losing games in training, and hated team mates misplacing passes. This mild mannered Slovakian would let rip with swear words in broken English. I didn't like that as I felt it was my job to swear at the lads!. **Neil Lennon**

420. AFTER THE FAMOUS Scottish Cup Final against Rangers at Hampden which we won 1-0 with George McCluskey scoring the goal, I invited all the players back to my house for a party. Later that night there was a knock at the front door. I opened it and standing outside with their carry outs were Bobby Murdoch, Jimmy Johnstone, and Kenny Dalglish. Three of my heroes wanted to come to my party! **Frank McGarvey.**

421. WHEN I FIRST signed for Celtic I thought that I was fit. I had been a full time professional for six years and looked after myself. But the fitness levels of the Celtic playes was incredible and it took me about three months to get up to speed. **Evan Willams** who was signed from Wolves. He replaced Lisbon Lion Ronnie Simpson. Evan had a good record of shut outs when playing against Rangers.

422. THE HIGH POINT of my career was signing for Celtic. My best goal was my first against Rangers. My favourite player was Kenny Dalglish. My favourite stadium is Celtic Park. My favourite other team is Celtic reserves. **Mo Johnstone** writing in the club programme after he signed for Celtic. (the first time)

423. IN 1998 CELTIC signed Australian born centre forward **Mark Viduka** from Croatia Zagreb. He played 48 games for Celtic and scored 35 goals.

424. THEY TALK ABOUT Pele, Maradona, Cruyff, but for me Jimmy Johnstone was the best. When I heard the news that he had died, I wore a black tie for two days. **Eusebio**

425. IT'S NOT RELIGION that's the problem - it's the lack of religion. **Jock Stein**

426. ONE OF MY greatest childhood memories is Celtic winning the European Cup. For weeks before the game my Dad had us saying in our prayers " God Bless Jock Stein and Jimmy Johnstone". **Pauline Dunlop**

427. "THEY ARE NOT rules for only Christmas and New Year, they are guidelines for as long as I am here. I just want to say 'listen, this is what I think is best for you'. They are not for my benefit, because I don't go out. They can come and watch telly with me if they want, as long as it's not Scott Brown. They can all come apart

from him." Celtic manager **Gordon Strachan** advised his squad to stay away from nightlife venues in Glasgow.

428. IF A PLAYER cannot turn and accelerate quickly enough over three yards he becomes susceptible to what **Jock Stein** once called " dustbin defending."

429. LISBON LION **JOHN Clark** was signed by Birmingham City a few weeks before he joined Celtic. But there was a dispute about the amount of money to be paid to his junior club, Larkhall Thistle, and the deal was cancelled. He signed for Celtic 1958. At that time the Celtic reserves played on a Friday night. John would play in these games, and the next day he would pay his own bus fare and admission money to go and watch the first team.

430. ON THE 12 December 2008 Celtic unveiled a memorial statue in honour of **Jimmy Johnstone,** the man voted the club's Greatest Ever Player. The statue is positioned at the main entrance to Celtic Park. The sculptor was Kate Robinson, who also created the statue at Celtic Park of the club's founder Brother Walfrid. She said that when she was creating the statue of Jimmy she wanted to express movement, focus, energy, determination, as well as a sense of the future.

431. CELTIC LEGEND **BOBBY Lennox** broke his leg at Ibrox after a tackle by Rangers hard man John Greig. Bobby was asked later when did he realise it was a fracture. " When I saw it was John Greig coming over to tackle me"

432. THE NIGHT THAT Inverness Caledonian Thistle beat Celtic 3-1 at Celtic Park was big news. Later that night on the national " News at Ten" TV channel across the UK, it was the second lead story. Celtic are always big news. The next day manager John Barnes was sacked.

433. **Séamus John James "Shay" Given** was a young goalkeeper signed by Celtic manager Liam Brady in 1991. Shay joined the club he supported. He spent two years at Celtic and despite being named on the substitutes bench for the Old Firm derby against Rangers on 1 January 1994, he never played in the first team. The next Celtic manager, Lou Macari, let him go at the end of the season in 1994. One of the rumours flying around Glasgow at that time was that Given's contract was lying in the manager's bottom drawer and he forgot all about it. Shay went onto have great career in England and with the Republic of Ireland at international level.

434. "I was so happy to have played my greatest game against Rangers on such an occasion." **Jimmy Johnstone** after he inspired Celtic to beat Rangers 2-1 in the Scottish Cup Final replay in 1971. It was a tense match played on a Wednesday evening at Hampden. Jinky stayed up to 3 o'clock the next morning playing records with his wife, and then took the dog for a walk at five o'clock.

435. I want my players to hate losing so much so that their weekend becomes painful if it happens. After a defeat I don't expect players to come into training with a smile on their faces, and joking about a match that we have lost. I want to see a determination to make amends in the next game. **Martin O'Neill**.

436. The most important thing for me was the reaction from my team-mates. Almost everyone came to celebrate with me – even our goalkeeper Artur Boruc who ran from the other end of the field. I was very happy and it was a proud moment for me. Celtic's Japanese player **Koki Mizuno** after scoring his first goal for Celtic against Falkirk in a 3-0 win on 21December 2008.

437. " I have been involved in football all my life, and I have never experienced anything like the visit from the Celtic fans. What a bunch of great people. Even in defeat they were gracious and

friendly. You say we have started a Celtic Supporters Club here in Villareal, but that is not true. Your supporters started the Villareal CSC by the way they showed themselves to us". President of Spanish team Villareal

438. CELTIC'S JAPANESE PLAYER **Shunsuke Nakamura** always changed his boots at half time if it was raining. He did not like playing in wet boots and always freshened up at half time.

439. **HENRIK LARSSON** PRODUCED great performances every week – he was so consistent. The Man of the Match award became something of a joke, because it became the Man of the Match (as long as you don't include Henrik) competition.

440. IT IS STILL the proudest day of my life, much better than my telegram from the Queen last year. Celtic supporter **Jock Hagen** talking in 2008 when he was 101 years old. Jock lived in Portadown in Ireland. He turned 60 years old just after Celtic won the European Cup in 1967.

441. CELTIC BEAT MORTON 8-1 on Christmas Day 1965 at Celtic Park. They were up 7-0 at half time. **Joe McBride** scored three goals. It was a good festive period for Celtic. A week later on 03 January 1966 they beat Rangers 5-1 at Celtic Park.

442. I AM PROUD to be part of Celtic football club and the history. I am not the first German unfortunately, Andreas Thom was here before me, but I am very proud to play for Celtic. **Andreas Hinkel**. When he signed for Celtic he read a number of books on the history of Celtic.

443. " THE BA just hit ma heid " **John Hughes**. The Celtic centre half scored the equaliser against Rangers in the 1-1 draw at Ibrox on 17 March 1996. What a way to celebrate St.Patrick's Day

444. CELTIC BEAT ENGLISH champions Liverpool in 1989 to win the Dubai Cup. The trophy has never been played for again and it is still at Celtic Park.

445. MY ADVICE TO any young player who wants to play for Celtic is to be humble. You can get carried away with all the hype that surrounds football in Glasgow. It is difficult for some people to handle. **Marc Reiper**, the Danish internationalist who played for Celtic in the late 1990's.

446. I WANT TO be a legend here, it is as simple as that. I want to be held in high esteem when I leave this club. You have to do your talking on the pitch at Celtic. **Neil Lennon**

447. I LIKE HAGGIS but I can't eat too much of it or I'll get fat. Now and again it is okay though. Sheep's insides, right? I don't mind that. **Shunsuke Nakamura** talks about Scottish food.

448. SEVENTY THREE CELTIC players have represented Glasgow in the annual inter city game against Sheffield. The first game was at Bramall Lane in 1874, and the final game was at Celtic Park in 1960.

449. IN SEASON 1904/05 Celtic and Rangers were tied on 41 points each after 26 games. Goal average and goal difference were not the method to decide who would win the league, so the SFA decided to play a league decider at Hampden. An English referee, Mr.Kirkham, was brought up for the game. Celtic won 2-1.

450. IF I AM out shopping in Glasgow fans might ask for an autograph or something. Back home in Japan people follow me and take pictures or videos with camera phones. So maybe for that reason it's a bit easier to go out when living abroad. Going out for noodles in Tokyo or Yokohama might prove a bit difficult. But as long as my family aren't bothered it's not so bad. **Shunsuke Nakamura.** Naka can be seen on the television advertising energy drinks,

on the metro promoting magazines, or in sports shops endorsing clothing brands in Japan. He is very popular.

451. THE RUNNERS RUN, the workers work, and the players play. **Jock Stein**. Every player had a role to play in the team.

452. AT CELTIC IF you have two draws in a row there is talk of a crisis. **Paul Lambert**.

453. THERE IS NEVER a dull moment at Celtic Football Club. The next massive piece of news will probably be only around the corner. **Gordon Strachan**

454. I LOVED THE responsibility of playing for Celtic, but I loved winning more. **Neil Lennon**

455. I AM JUST a Celtic fan who got lucky. **Tommy Burns**.

456. " HE IS too much of a supporter to be the manager" description in fanzine of **Billy McNeill**

457. **BOBBY EVANS** WAS voted Scotland' Player of the Year in 1953. It was said that his enthusiasm and spirit was worth a goal in any match. He was the first Celtic captain to lift the League Cup above his head in 1956 when Celtic beat Partick Thistle 3-0 in the final at Hampden. (it was a replay as the first game had been a 0-0 draw). The goal scorers were Billy McPhail (2) and Bobby Collins. Evans was such a consistent player during his Celtic career that the weekly newspapers used to say, " Evans, as usual, was superb" when reporting on Celtic games.

458. TOMMY BURNS WAS simply one of the best friends anyone could ever hope to have. I can only consider myself fortunate not only to have worked with him on a daily basis for the past three years but to have been able to count him as a friend. He made me understand what Glasgow was about. If I hadn't had him I'd have

gone off my head. **Gordon Strachan** after the death of Tommy Burns.

459. You GET OLDER, you learn your lessons, the penny drops. I told him from day one that players get kicked and have their jerseys pulled and you should take it as a compliment - it's a fact, it happens to all good players. You've got to learn to deal with it in a positive way, not the negative. The positive way is to smile and get on with it and score goals, win the game for your team. The negative is to argue and get booked and get ruffled. Ex Celt **John Collins** gives advice to Scott Brown.

460. **HENRIK LARSSON** PLAYED three games for Celtic reserves and scored three goals.

461. THE GAME WAS 90 minutes long, but for me the game lasted as long as my five years as captain and our six years without a trophy. **Paul McStay** after Celtic beat Airdrie 1-0 in the Scottish Cup final in 1995.

462. " I HEARD you got fired !" **Henrik Larsson** signed the Hoop jersey of a Celtic fan named Danny J. He worked in a Call Centre (owned by Rangers chairman David Murray), but when Celtic played Boavista in Portugal in the UEFA Cup Semi Final he phoned in sick, and went to the game. Unfortunately he was pictured celebrating in the crowd by a photographer at the game, and his face was plastered on the back page of every newspaper in Scotland. He got fired from his job.

463. CAN YOU IMAGINE your life without Celtic – I mean what would you do with your weekends? **Pub football expert.**

464. " MR.LAWWELL YOU may be the Chief Executive of Celtic Football Club, but I am the Chief Executive of Bobo Balde." Celtic centre half **Bobo Balde** comment to the Celtic Chief Executive during a meeting to negotiate his salary.

465. **BOBBY MURDOCH** PLAYED the European Cup Final in Lisbon with only one good foot. An Inter Milan player stood on his right foot very early in the game and he felt a searing pain. There was no substitutes on the bench (apart from goalkeeper John Fallon) and he had to play on. Bobby played the game with his left foot, and was the best player on the park. Bertie Auld remembers looking at Murdochs ankle during the first half and could see it swelling up. " I don't like the look of that" said Bertie to his colleague. " I am not too chuffed myself " was the reply from Murdoch.

466. AS A YOUNG player Lisbon Lion **Bertie Auld** played in the same team as Jock Stein, Sean Fallon, and Neilly Mochan. They went on to be the management team that lead Celtic to win the European Cup.

467. LISBON LION GOALKEEPER **Ronnie Simpson's** father, Jimmy, played for Rangers. He was centre half the day Johnny Thomson was fatally injured in the game at Ibrox in 1931. Ronnie's father was so upset about that day that he seldom mentioned it again to his son.

468. IN 1972 A Hungarian Professor of sport, Arpad Csandi, wrote a superb book covering all aspects of football. Two points he made have stuck in my memory. (a). The best tactical plan can fail if the physical conditioning of the players is left out of the consideration. (b). the purpose of the game cannot be achieved by attack alone. At certain stages of a match even the best teams may be compelled to play a defensive game. Lisbon Lion **Jim Craig**.

469. THAT WAS A stupid thing to do. **Jock Stein** to Jim Craig as he was taken off after breaking his nose in a game against Finnish team Kokkula in 1970.

470. IN 2004 CELTIC signed Brazilian World Cup winner Oswaldo Goroldi Junior, otherwise known as **Juninho.** He made his de-

but in the 1-0 win over Rangers at Celtic Park. Alan Thompson scored the winner.

471. IN 2004 CELTIC fan **Tony Allan** won a competition to commentate on an Old Firm game. (Celtic won 1-0). " Before the game I had been a bit worried about getting carried away and swearing into the microphone, and I have to admit I did let it slip out. That Rangers player Alex Rae did something and maybe I called him something that I shouldn't have.!"

472. THE DAY THAT **John Collins** was signing for Celtic from Hibs in 1990, Rangers called at his door at 7am in the morning with a lucrative contract to join them. John refused.

473. ONE OF THE goals of the **North American Federation of Celtic Supporters Clubs** (NAFCSC) when it was formed in the mid 1990's was: " that wherever any Celtic supporter goes in North America there will be a Celtic club or pub where he or she can drop in and enjoy watching the Bhoys along with fellow Celts". At the Las Vegas Convention in 1997, the Lisbon Lions attended. Two of the founders of the NAFCSC, Jacky Meehan and Tommy Donnelly, were presented with blazers and appointed Honourary Lisbon Lions for their outstanding work!

474. BIG JOCK WOULDN'T compliment his players much, but he had a knack of getting them to believe that they were the best. Before he came we were probably too nice. Jock was the first manager to tell us, " if there is a 50/50 ball, then you must win it". **Bertie Auld.**

475. "YOU ARE REALLY going mental when you are having arguments with people who are not even here." **Gordon Strachan** on (false) accusations that he had a fall out with ex-Celtic player Paul Telfer, who had left the club a month ago.

476. I SAY THINGS and I say them tongue-in-cheek, I don't have a problem with people having opinions as long as it's done in a respectful manner. I just like good manners. **Gordon Strachan.**

477. THE BEST BUY of the 1960's was when Celtic signed **Bertie Auld** from Birmingham City for £12,000. **Pub football expert**

478. "WHO NEEDS ALL that running about? A thirty yard pass can do all the damage that you want." **Bobby Murdoch** who always made sure the ball did the work.

479. THE THAIS LOVE their football. In the stalls in the markets in Bangkok, Celtic jerseys take their place amongst the jerseys from Real Madrid, Liverpool, Arsenal, and Manchester United. The Celtic strip is the only Scottish kit being sold. **Colin Mackin,** who travelled across the Far East and watched the Celtic games in various bars and internet cafes.

480. "25% OF OUR [Celtic] managers have been Protestant!" **Jock Stein's** response on being appointed manager of Celtic: The headlines in the papers were that he was the first Protestant manager of Celtic (they neglected to say that he was only the 4th manager in the club's history).

481. THEY SAY THE attendance was 137,000 at Hampden Park that night – the game had been switched from Celtic Park to accommodate a bigger crowd. You will never see a game like that in Glasgow again. There was so much electricity in the atmosphere that you could have lit up the city with it. The noise from the crowd was frightening. It was the most enjoyable game of my life. I played in midfield with Murdoch and Auld that night. But Jinky was fantastic turning the Leeds United defence inside out. **George Connelly** on the semi final of the European Cup against Leeds in 1970. Celtic won 2-1.

482. "WHEN WE GATHERED for the first meeting the next season (after winning the European Cup in 1967), Jock said, 'For some of you football will never be the same again.' He wanted to provoke us into proving him wrong, but it turned out to be right." **Bobby Murdoch**

483. "IF THEY WERE interested in what I had to say they would get here in time. The door stays shut!" **Jock Stein** on barring late journalists to his press talks.

484. HE IS THE best left back in the world. Jock Stein talking about **Tommy Gemmell**

485. "IF YOU'RE GOOD enough, the referee doesn't matter." **Jock Stein**

486. AN EXTRAORDINARY FACT in connection with the start of Celtic is that not a man among the founders knew anything about the practical side of football. None had every played the game. Yet in the first year of the club's life, Celts were within an ace of winning the Scottish Cup. **Willie Maley**

487. CELTIC BEAT RANGERS 4-0 in the 1969 Scottish Cup Final and George Connolly scored a great goal. That night we all went out for a drink in the Mauritania Hotel in Clackmannan. There was ten of us and later after a good drink we decided to go back to George's house in Kincardine. About three o'clock in the morning we decided to go outside for a game of football. A neighbour phoned the police. The policeman arrived and asked what was going on: he looked around and saw George Connolly, Davie Hay, John Gorman, Jimmy Quinn, and me. He asked for our autographs! **Davie Cattenach.** He played for Celtic in the 1960's and was a member of the Celtic squad in Lisbon in 1967.

488. THERE WAS A fad in Glasgow when raising money for Charity, to organise football celebrities to have a boxing match. **Chic**

Charnley, who played for Partick Thistle but was a huge Celtic fan, was asked who he would like to fight in the ring. " Mo Johnston" was the answer. Luckily for Mo, the fight never happened!

489. IN OCTOBER 1967 Celtic beat Dundee 5-3 in the League Cup Final at Hampden. Hughes, Lennox, Wallace and Chalmers (2), scored the goals. Immediately after the game the players went to Prestwick Airport to catch their flight to Argentina for the World Club Championship game against Racing Club. It was a long journey with stops in Paris, Madrid and Rio de Janeiro. The exhausted players arrived in Buenos Aires after a 21hour journey.

490. FOR ME DANNY McGrain epitomised everything good about Celtic. I played against Celtic greats like big Billy McNeil, Bertie Auld, and Tommy Gemmell, but playing alongside Danny, seeing how he went about his business every day, was a delight. The one player who summed up Celtic for me was Danny. **Pat Stanton** who signed for Celtic from Hibs in 1976 aged 32 years old.

491. IT IS EASIER to play against the Old Firm than it is to play for them. **Tommy Burns** explains why it often takes new players time to adjust to playing for Celtic.

492. THE MANAGER HAS instilled an unbelievable confidence in the team. He makes you play better and he makes you want to win. He has a real will to win and has transmitted this to all the players. **Paul Lambert** talking about manager Martin O'Neill after Celtic beat Rangers 6-2.

493. IN THE 1960's Celtic played against Arbroath at their park, which is next to the North Sea, in league games. The biggest danger was not from the Arbroath players, but the spray from the sea if it was a windy day, or being hit by a flying Smokie.

494. **SHUNSUKE NAKAMURAS** BRILLIANCE from dead-ball situations is well documented . When Celtic were awarded a free-kick just outside the penalty area against Dundee United in the 2-2 draw at Celtic Park in January 2009, United manager Craig Levein decided to do something different. " He's brilliant at getting the ball up and over a wall, so we didn't have one. I shouted to our captain Lee Wilkie to put a man on the right-hand post , and the rest of our players took up positions in and around the six-yard box, just picking up any Celtic player in the area. The idea was to create a little bit of confusion and uncertainty in Nakamura's mind.". Naka did not score from this one.

495. **JOHN JACK** WAS the centre half in the first Celtic team to win the Scottish League Cup in October 1956. (the first official season of the League Cup was 1946/47, so Celtic had to wait a long time until they won this trophy). Celtic beat Partick Thistle 3-0 in a replay after the first game ended 0-0. John came from Bellshill and had been born named Jonas Kaduskeviechi, but he decided to change his name. He was a strong player who played 68 times for Celtic.

496. **PLAYERS WHO WANT** to play for Celtic must be protected against those who don't. Success affects people in different ways, not always for the best. **Jock Stein** talking about bad influences in the dressing room.

497. **JOHN ROBERT "JACKIE" McNamara** signed for Celtic in 1995 from Dunfermline. Jackie was a terrific player who played for Celtic for 10 years. To reward his loyalty, Celtic played a testimonial match against the Republic of Ireland. The match ended 1-0 to Ireland. Jackie used to have the players in stitches of laughter when he did his impression of the characters from the popular TV comedy "Chewin The Fat". When he left Celtic he gave a computer to every player who played in his testimonial as a gift, with a screensaver of his face!

498. LISTEN SON, IBROX was built from bricks baked in Hell, and sitting in the dressing room tomorrow the Celtic players will feel like they are in the Devils Lair. But class always tells, and if Henrik and Lubo play well we will win by a few goals, no worries. **Pub football expert**

499. I WISH SOME of our players had the same spirit as the supporters. Celtic manager **Billy McNeill** talking in 1978.

500. CELTIC MANAGER **GORDON Strachan** was a top player. He was named Scottish Footballer of the Year in 1979-80. He started his career as a player at Dundee. The story goes that he was playing in a reserve game, and the opposition had a set of twins playing. One of them fouled Strachan. He wasn't sure which one it was, so he punched both of them. Gordon had a quick temper.

501. **WILLIE O'NEILL** WAS the regular left back (Gemmell was right back) for Celtic in the great season 1966/67, but lost his place in the team to Jim Craig after the 3-2 defeat to Dundee United at the New Year. Willie was a great friend of Jimmy Johnstone and Bobby Lennox. It was said that it was Willie's humour that kept Jinky laughing during plane trips for away games in Europe. (Jinky hated flying).

502. **JIMMY JOHNSTONE** WAS at such a low ebb in 1965 that it was probable that he would revert to playing in Junior football, and sink without trace. Cyril Horne, sports reporter writing in the Glasgow Herald. Things changed for the better for all the players when Jock Stein became the Celtic manager.

503. THE CELTIC TEAM that beat St.Mirren 5-0 on 03 May 1986 to win the league on the last day of the season was Bonner, McGrain, Whyte, Aitken, McGugan, MacLeod, McClair, McStay, Johnston, Burns and Archdeacon. Peter Grant was on the bench.

504. I REMEMBER ASKING Alex McNair, who played 21 years for us and who was a great student of the game, how he maintained his interest in football. He told me " I've never seen match yet that's not got something new in it" **Sir Robert Kelly**, chairman of Celtic.

505. PORTUGESE STRIKER **JORGE Cadete** was a goal machine for Celtic. He scored 38 goals in only 43 games (plus five as a sub). Unfortunately the cold wet climate of Glasgow did not suit him or his family, and he was transferred to Celta Vigo in Spain in August 1997 for £3 million pounds.

506. CELTIC PARK NOW is like paradise compared to the old days. I remember freezing Saturday afternoons in The Jungle watching poor Celtic teams, and where the only hope of any heat was if some fan with a poor aim missed the beer can and mistakenly pee'd doon the back of your legs. **Pub football expert**

507. MALKY MACKAY WAS just five metres from me but I could not hear what he was shouting because the noise was so loud. For the first time in my life I could feel the noise going right through my body. When we scored the singing got louder and I actually had goosepimples and the hairs on the back of my neck stood up. **Stephane Mahe** describes the atmosphere the night Celtic beat Tirol 6-3 at Celtic Park in August 1997. He was the first Frenchman to play for Celtic.

508. IF YOU TALK about the Old Firm, I think it is the biggest derby in the world. Nothing else even comes close to it. I've played 'El Classico' in Barcelona against Real Madrid and it's a nice game, but it doesn't reach the same noise level as you get in Glasgow. **Henrik Larsson**

509. SOMETHING ALWAYS COMES out which makes the rivalry more intense. **Martin O'Neill** says he learned to discard stories in newspapers on the countdown to a meeting with Rangers.

510. IN MY ENTIRE career at Celtic Park, we were never once told what our bonus would be for winning a cup-tie, either at home or in Europe. We knew what the league bonuses were, because we picked them up every week. But for the cups, we were never told, and that applied in Lisbon, as well. I think big Dessie [Desmond White the Celtic club secretary] waited to see who we had drawn in the next round and calculated what it would be worth before our bonus was determined. **Tommy Gemmell**

511. WHEN I CAME to Celtic I think players expected me to be more aggressive because they had seen me on the television playing for my other clubs. I think they were surprised that I wasn't that fiery. **John Hartson**.

512. IN 1947 CELTIC played Belfast Celtic in Ireland during a pre season game. After twenty minutes Belfast were winning 4-0, and one of their players, **Charlie Tully**, was causing havoc. The game eventually finished 4-4, but Charlie had impressed the Celtic manager Jimmy McGrory. Not long afterwards he signed Charlie.

513. IN THE EARLY 1900's the **Glasgow Observer** newspaper loved the Celtic football team, and was notorious for its bias towards them when reporting on games.

514. IN 1967 **CHARLIE Gallagher** was appointed captain for the day when Celtic played Elgin City in a Scottish Cup game at Celtic Park. Charlie had been selected earlier that week by the Republic of Ireland for game against Turkey, and Big Jock Stein marked this special occasion for Charlie by making him Celtic captain for the day.

515. **JOHN HARTSON** FAILED a medical when Ranger wanted to sign him. This was Celtic's gain. Big John went onto score 8 goals for Celtic in his games against Rangers.

516. " **Martin O'Neill's** players do not surround referees and question their decisions. Handling Rangers games is like taking up a poison chalice." An anonymous "top Scottish referee" quoted in a weekend newspaper.

517. It was great. I was in primary seven at school and so it was special to fly to Paris to play against some of the best players in the world. We played against Brazil, and it was great to represent Scotland. **Aiden McGeady**. When he was twelve years old, Aiden was selected to play in a mini tournament before the World Cup started in France in 1998.

518. Celtic played Manchesetr United (with many of the Busby Babes) at Celtic Park in April 1956. This was a charity game organised by Viscount Cheshire. He was a war hero who founded homes for the old and poor. During the game the Celtic goalkeeper Dick Beattie was injured, and there was no substitute keeper. John Bonnar was in the stand, and he had to rush down and get changed and then take his place in goal.

519. He doesn't do badly for an ugly bloke. **Martin O'Neill** on Neil Lennon after the Celtic midfielder turns up with a mystery brunette after a players' Christmas party.

520. In season 2005/06, Celtic signed Chinese defender **Du Wei** on a 6 month loan spell. He was a former captain of China's U-21 Team and China's Olympic team in 2004. He was described by Maradona, who watched him in action at the 2001 World Youth Championship in Argentina, as having unparalleled speed and a keen sense of how to defend. He made his debut for Celtic in the Scottish Cup Third Round tie against Clyde on 9 January 2006 in a surprise 2-1 defeat. Du was substituted at half time by manager Gordon Strachan. He played no more games for the first team and was soon released.

521. " Give me joy in my heart Henrik Larsson, Give me joy in my heart I pray Give me joy in my heart Henrik Larsson, Give me Larsson until the end of day Henrik Larsson, Henrik Larsson, Henrik Larsson, Is the King of Kings." Celtic supporters chant to **Henrik Larsson**.

522. I could never sleep the night before an Old Firm game. I would toss and turn and kick every ball in my bed. When the game started I would always look for a team mate to put in a strong tackle early on. That would give me confidence, and although I knew I could expect a kick or two, I always enjoyed the game, as long as we won. **Jimmy Johnstone**

523. The Tommy Burns Supper is the Herriot Watt & Edinburgh Universities Celtic Supporters Club primary annual social evening. It has developed over the years into one of the best-known events on the Celtic social calendar. Like the far-inferior Rabbie Burns Supper, on which it is loosely based, it has acquired its own set of traditions, which are fiercely guarded by the club, Celebrated speakers include Frank McAvennie, Neil Lennon, Tom Boyd, Danny McGrain, and Billy McNeill. www.hweucsc.net

524. If chairman Bob Kelly said " Good Morning" to you at Celtic Park then you knew you were playing. If he walked past you without saying a word then you knew that you were not playing on Saturday. **Charlie Gallagher**. In 1950's and early 1960's it was chairman Kelly who picked the team.

525. Jinky was as hard as nails. When I was a fifteen year old on the Celtic ground staff, he would come down to the gym, give me a medicine ball and ask me to bounce it off his stomach. I didn't like too at first in case I hurt him. But he would just lie there and I would bounce it off his belly!. His muscles were strong. He was a tough wee fella. **George Connelly** talking about Jimmy Johnstone.

526. JOCK STEIN INJURED his ankle against Rangers in 1955 and the injury eventually caused him to retire from playing football. He took over coaching of the Celtic reserves. In 1958 the reserves beat Rangers 8-2 on aggregate to win the reserves XI cup.

527. HE IS THE kind of player who, when he did not know what to do with the ball, he sticks it in the net. Jock Stein talking about **Joe McBride**

528. " I AM glad to see **Peter Grant** is now getting a regular game for Celtic. I think he should be offered a new contract." This letter appeared in the Not the View fanzine letters page in May 1993. It was submitted by a Peter Grant, London Road, Glasgow.

529. PLAYING AGAINST HIM you need shinguards on the back of your head. **Bertie Auld** talking about Bobby Shearer who was the captain of Rangers in the early 1960's.

530. TOMMY GEMMELL WAS playing against Rangers right winger Willie Henderson in an Old Firm game. Henderson was a good player but very short sighted. He heard a shout coming from the dugout during a game. He said to big Tam – " where is the dugout?" – Big Tam of course lead him across to the Celtic dugout. Wee Henderson shouted in " What is it you want me to do ?" – Big Tam had a good laugh.

531. NOT ONLY HAS the support encouraged the team, but I would say that, 100%, our support has won games for us: and it is our duty as officials of this club, to make sure that the future for our supporters is a future which should be a winning Celtic team and not only being the best in Scotland, but in comparison with the best in Europe. **Jock Stein** speaking in 1967

532. "THIS WONDERFUL FOOTBALLER who achieves his purpose without the merest suggestion of relying on the physical, and who suffers the crude, unfair attempts to stop him without a thought of retali-

ation." The Glasgow Herald newspaper describes Celtic's **Willie Fernie** after the 7–1 victory over Rangers

533. AS PART OF an anti-sectarianism campaign, Alistair Devine has put the call out for volunteers to participate in the " Stripped Naked " project which will show nude Rangers and Celtic supporters frolicking together on the pitch. The hundreds of fans, both male and female, will only be covered by their club's scarves. Mr Devine said: "Following on from the iconic image I captured in 1980 which highlighted all that is bad about the game and portrayed Scotland in a negative light, I am now going to capture what will be an iconic image of serious relevance to where Scotland as a country and a footballing nation is today." The appeal is for participants aged over 18 and "of any shape or size". 03 September 2007.

534. SAINT PETER WAS manning the Pearly Gates when forty **Rangers** fans showed up. Never having seen any **Rangers** supporters at Heaven's door, Saint Peter said he would have to check with God. After hearing the news, God instructed him to admit the ten most virtuous from the group. A few minutes later, Saint Peter returned to God breathless and said, "They're gone." "What? All of the **Rangers** fans are gone?" asked God. "No" replied Saint Peter "**The Pearly Gates!**" www.fannation.com

535. HE WAS SO combative, like a little flyweight boxer. He would kill his mother for a result. Leeds and England centre half Jack Charlton talking about **Bobby Collins**. When Bobby was at Celtic he was nick named " Lester" after the champion jockey Lester Piggot, who was small but renowned for his dedication and determination. Bobby had the same spirit and resented losing a football game.

536. **BILLY MCNEILL** USED to have a pub in the South side of Glasgow. One night he offered to go out for some fish suppers for his regu-

lars. One of his regulars is alleged to have shouted: " Don't you go Billy. The last time you went shopping you brought back Martin Hayes !" (Billy paid £650,000 to sign Hayes from Arsenal. But he was not a success at Celtic.)

537. I THINK EVERYONE under estimated the impact that Celtic could have, even Celtic themselves. The same allure is not there for Rangers. We tried it last year and it didn't work. The Irish factor makes Celtic a different matter and for me they are under estimating their brand. They should invest more time in this country. **Georgio Chinaglia** speaking on behalf of sponsors who organise friendly games in America.

538. " THERE ARE certain coaches you feel that you are in tune with and that is how I feel about Wim Jansen. I would walk on fire for him." **Regi Blinker** when he signed for Celtic in 1997 from Sheffield Wedensday. Regi was born in Surinam and had played in Holland for Feyenoord (along side Henrik Larsson) when Wim Jansen was the manager.

539. THE DIRTIEST, UGLIEST game of football I have even seen was the game against Atletico Madrid at Celtic Park in the semi final of the European Cup. The Spaniards were brutal. The Celtic Board gave the Celtic players a special bonus (even although they did not win), because the players were so well behaved and did not retaliate to the assaults on them. **Pub football expert**

540. **BOBBY COLLINS** WAS known as " The Wee Barra" because he was only 5' 4" tall, but he was a tough player who scored 117 goals for Celtic. Celtic chairman Robert Kelly told manager Jimmy McGrory not to pick Collins for the Scottish Cup Final replay in 1955 against Clyde because he was not pleased about a strong challenge Collins had made on the Clyde goalkeeper in the first game. Celtic lost the replay 1-0.

541. IN FEBRUARY 2007 Celtic's Dutch striker **Jan Vennegoor of Hesselink** was sent off in a game at Inverness for celebrating a goal with the Celtic fans. He was given a yellow card. (he had already received a yellow card early in the game). The referee could have shown some common sense when the goal was scored: the fans are very close behind the goals at Inverness, and it is difficult for players not to celebrate with them.

542. "A LIFETIME AMBITION is being fulfilled today." Simple Minds singer **Jim Kerr** (a great Celtic supporter) in the recording studio just before he started recording/singing Dirty Old Town with Jimmy Johnstone

543. MY FIRST MEMORY of Jinky is him dribbling around big defenders. I thought everyone played football like him. Then I realised he was unique. **Charlie Burchill** from the Simple Minds band.

544. IN THE 1967 European Cup Final in Lisbon Celtic had a remarkable 23 efforts on goal from outside the penalty area.! Celtic's shooting power from outside the 18 yard line was legendary.

545. MY HEART USED to sink and I was filled with dread whenever that wee man trotted onto the field. Campbell Ogilvie, who became secretary of Rangers, talking about **Jimmy Johnstone.**

546. JIMMY JOHNSTONE LIKED to sing. He would sing his songs to anyone who listened. He would entertain the team for hours. He had a good voice. **Billy McNeill**

547. I STARTED TO support Celtic after I met Jock Stein in the early 1970's (I was introduced by Kenny Dalglish). Once you meet Jock you never forget it. He made football sound like poetry. I was hooked. I have been a Celtic supporter ever since then. **Rod Stewart** (Why I support Celtic on www.youtube.com)

548. IN THE EARLY 1970's we used to drive 2 hours up the 401 highway to watch a reel-to- reel film of the previous weeks game. We

had to wait until the Wednesday to read the Toronto papers to get the Celtic result, nae phones in the family at hame. **Charlie McGregor**, Celtic supporter in Canada.

549. IN JANUARY 2009 **Scott Brown** was named one of FIFA's stars of the future. FIFA listed the midfielder as one of their 'stars set to shine in 2009" along with Brazilians Douglas, Keirrison, Michel Fernandes, Pedro Tonon Geromel and Manchester United's Rafael da Silva. He was described as " Direct, athletic and combative Brown has thrived after successfully curbing a reckless streak that blighted last season, his first at Celtic since his 4.5 million pounds move from Hibernian."

550. " IF YOU had a boot on your heid, you would be the best full back the world has ever seen or ever will see." Celtic's Neil McCallum to his team mate **Jack "Baldy" Reynolds.** Reynolds was signed from Aston Villa in 1893 and it was said he could header a ball, which took a lot of courage in those days, further than he could kick it. Jack went onto work with Ajax in Amsterdam in the 1920's

551. THE GUYS IN the dressing room didn't know what he was going through towards the end of last season. Broonie was getting stick from some people for his displays when nobody knew what was going on in his personal life. That must have been an incredibly hard thing to do and shows the strength of his character. He managed to protect himself and his family while helping us to win the championship. I can't speak highly enough about him. Celtic captain **Stephen McManus** talking about his team mate **Scott Brown**, who played season 2008 while keeping his sister's terminal illness to himself.

552. I HAVE SYMPATHY for Artur (Boruc). When you make a mistake for Celtic (or Rangers) it's the loneliest place in the world and I wouldn't wish it on my worst enemy. Ex Celtic goalkeeper

Rab Douglas talking after Boruc mis-kicked a ball that allowed Dundee to take the lead in the Scottish Cup game against Dundee at Celtic Park in January 2009. Celtic eventually won 2-1.

553. The next generation of players coming along are mercenaries, interested only in how much money they will get for playing, rather than who they will play for, and how much they will lend themselves to the team once they get on the park. **Tommy Burns** in 1989.

554. **Paul McStay** was a fantastic passer of a football. In the New Years day game against Rangers in 1989 he turned in the middle of the park, had a good look around the park, then sent a forty yard pass down the wing to full back Chris Morris who crossed for Frank McAvennie to score. It was a moment of brilliance and awareness. McStay was often marked by two men in a game, and he was encouraged to get his passes going rather than taking people on all the time. He was nicknamed The Maestro and was a credit to Celtic.

555. **Neilly Mochan** signed for Celtic on the eve of the Coronation Cup tournament in 1953. His first game was against Queens Park at Hampden in the Charity Shield final that Celtic won. His next three games were also at Hampden in the Coronation Cup when Celtic beat Arsenal, Manchester United, and then Hibs in the final. He had two winners medals before he ever appeared at Celtic Park. Neilly also played in the 7-1 game against Rangers, and was also the trainer of the Lisbon Lions.

556. For years nobody twigged that what we were doing, and looking for, was creating space. **Bobby Murdoch** talking about one of the keys to Celtic's success.

557. At the start of season 1971/72 Celtic played Rangers three times in five weeks at Ibrox. (Two League Cup games and a league game). The stand roof at Celtic Park was under construction, and

Celtic Park could not be used. A young **Kenny Dalglish** payed in all three games and scored in each game. Celtic won all the games. 2-0, 3-0, and 3-2.

558. I WAS STILL a part time player at Celtic. Big Jock Stein used to train us in the evening in his early years at Celtic. After training was finished, he used to go home on the bus with us. Myself, Jim Conway and John Clark would stand at the same bus stop as him, but Big Jock's bus would go a different route from ours into Lanarkshire. The deal was that if his bus came first, he went on, but if our bus came first ,we stayed with him!   And then a while later, he got his own car and he used to drop us home, and it was great because we heard all his stories about his own career. He was a massive influence on all our careers. **Billy McNeill**.

559. " HERE IN Glasgow is a city about the size of Detroit, and it drops dead at 9 pm. Why, over in Detroit that's just late afternoon; you start out to enjoy yourself about then." Jamaican **Gilbert 'Gillie' Heron** signed for Celtic in 1951. He arrived in Scotland from Detroit, where following a stint in the Canadian armed forces during the war, he worked in an auto plant painting cars, while playing football part time. "Glasgow Celtic was," said a thrilled Heron, "the greatest name in football to me." A sharp dresser with a well developed sense of personal style, Heron, according to writer Gerry Hassan, lit up dull, gray, post-war Glasgow with his zoot suits, broad brimmed hats and colourful shoes. He played 5 games for Celtic and scored 2 goals. www.iamcolourful.com/articles

560. THE YEAR HE spent with Celtic was the best of his life. **Gil Heron** wrote a poem about his time with Celtic called the "Great Ones". " I'll remember all the great ones/Those that I have seen/Those that I have played with/Who wore the white and green./There was Tully and Bobby Evans/No greater ones you'd see,/And Celtic

park was our haven/To win was our destiny." **Gil** published two
books of poetry.

561. "SELF PRAISE IN no honour." **Willie Fearnie**. Willie was described as "Scotland's Stanley Matthews.". He was a wonderful
ball playing inside forward who played for the Hoops for over 10
years. Willie scored the last goal in the 7-1 victory over Rangers
in 1957.

562. THE FIRST CELTIC committee in 1888 consisted of 16 men. Dr,
John Conway, John Glass, John O'Hara, Hugh Darnoch, Willie
Maley, J.M.Nelis, Tom Maley, M.Cairns, Joseph Shaughnessy,
Pat Welsh, Daniel Molloy, David Meikleham, John McDonald,
William McKillop, John McLaughlin and Joseph McGrory.

563. **FRANK MCAVENNIE** WAS often late for training. One Christmas
Eve, I called him into my office to deal with his latest breach of
the rules and fined him £500, which was a fair amount of money
20 years ago. Frank just turned and left the office. Within seconds,
the door was thrown open again and there he was. I thought,
'Uh-oh, here it comes'. What he said was, 'Sorry, boss, I forgot
– Merry Christmas!' and broke into that big smile of his. What
could you do with somebody like that? I had to wait until he
left before shaking my head and laughing myself. Celtic manager
Billy McNeill.

564. BERTIE AULD TOLD me off in training for running with the ball.
He said I was running thirty yards then passing it ten, instead of
passing it thirty and running ten. It was good advice. **George
Connelly**

565. THE FOOTBALL PITCH to him was a chessboard. He seldom if ever
troubled himself with the physical side of the game –he had no
need. Willie Maley talking about the great **Jimmy " Napoleon"
McMenemy,** who played for Celtic for 18 years.

566. THE LINK BETWEEN a man and the history of the club of which he is a player, manager, or director, is of little relevance. What matters is that he can make history while part of it. A journalist writing in the Glasgow Herald about **Fergus McCann** in 1997

567. WHEN CELTIC PLAYED Racing Club of Argentina in the third game of the World Club Championship, the game was played in Montevideo in Uruguay. The Celtic players stayed in the posh Victoria Plaza hotel. The Celtic players were warned about the high number of prostitutes who had been seen in the hotel to ensure no one got into a compromising situation before the Big game.

568. BIG JOCK WAS way ahead of his time with things like tactics and innovations. I was lucky I spent three and a half years working with him and I loved him. I remember asking why Jock never criticised players, and got my most important piece of advice. He asked why should he hurt a player's family by criticising him in public. All you do is make enemies of their cousins, uncles, aunties, mothers, pals, teachers and milkmen. So why do it? Sir Alex Ferguson talking about **Jock Stein**.

569. " THERE IS only one **Jorge Cadete**, he puts the ball in the netty. He's Portuguese he scores with ease, walking in a Cadete Wonderland" was a regular chant when Jorge played at Celtic. A few years after he stopped playing, he appeared on the Portuguese version of Celebrity Big Brother. He did not win, but he met his girl friend in there, and promised to take her to see Celtic!

570. THE CELTIC VIEW newspaper was started in 1965. The idea came from **Jack McGinn**. When he presented his idea to the Celtic Board they asked how much it would cost to set up. Jack calculated the cost would be six hundred pounds. The View became self supporting and never cost Celtic any more money. The first edition cost four pence, and sold 31,000 copies.

571. I WAS FOUR or five years old when my dad took me to a football pitch for the first time. It was on Montjoly beach, near Cayenne. By the end of the day I was bitten by the bug. I was so taken with the game that my dad had to pull in the reins to stop me going into over-drive. The beautiful thing about football is you can play anywhere but you aren't a true Guianan if you can't play it on the beach. The country's best teams train on sand. It's our culture. **Marc-Antoine Fortune** who was born in French Guiana,

572. **WILLIE O'NEILL** WAS Celtic's first ever substitute when he re-placed his great friend Jimmy Johnstone in a 1-0 league Cup win over St. Mirren at Love Street in September 1966.

573. CELTIC SIGNED GIANT Slovakian defender **Stanislav Varga** in 2003 from Sunderland. He suffered a horrific injury when he was at Sunderland and was rushed to hospital with a blocked artery in his leg. The surgeons thought that they would have to amputate his leg, but after four operations his leg was saved. Big Stan played really well for the Hoops for three years.

574. IN 1968-69 CELTIC beat Rangers 3-1 in the Glasgow Cup Final. Jock Stein played his " Quality Street " team that day. Stein played with three defenders at the back in that game, Dave Cattenach, George Connelly, and me. Jock was a very innovative manager. **Davie Hay.**

575. " WEEJIMMYJOHNS'ON WHAT a player he was. If he selt the full back a dummy, he had to pay to get back into the park. He was a one off, unique, a magician." **Pub football expert**

576. " JOHN, YOU may be 20 years old, but you have the legs of a 70 year old man." A vascular surgeon said to Celtic's **John Divers**, who always had trouble with circulation to his legs. John eventually retired at 28 years old. He played 232 games for Celtic between 1957-1966 and scored 102 goals. He was the son of John Divers

who played for Celtic between 1932-1945, and was the nephew of Patsy Gallacher.

577. HE IS A very private man, who tends to keep himself to himself away from the ground. But he is always smiling, always polite and always professional. You never see him here not working. He's always doing something, whether it's training or practising his skills. Celtic Manager **Gordon Strachan** talking about Japanese player **Shunsuke Nakamura.**

578. "I LOST HIM at the airport, even though he was supposed to be looking after me. I dozed off and when I awoke he had disappeared. He was impossible to find because everyone looked the same, lying there in a mass of green and white. I've since heard he's still in Seville." Anonymous Celtic fan who attended UEFA Cup Final in Seville, despite being off work with a broken leg, and returned home minus his brother.

579. THE FITNESS OF the Celtic players in the final was of a very high standard and an important factor in breaking down the resolute resistance of the Internazionale defence. **Kurt Tschenscher**, the German referee in the Lisbon European Cup final in 1967.

580. BOBBY MURDOCH WAS the vice captain of the Lisbon Lions.

581. TO BE HERE today at Celtic Park is very special. This place is very spiritual. To see the bust of Jock Stein and the painting of all the captains is fantastic. And the story of Brother Walfrid is very touching. I've been all over the world and they talk about Hollywood, but that is nothing – it's all make-believe. This is the real thing. I wish I stayed just round the corner so I could come here every week. Actor **PH Moriarty,** who played Hatchet Harry in the film Lock, Stock, and Two Smoking Barrels.

582. I CONSIDER IT a great honour to be asked to open the magnificent new stand. I look forward to joining fellow Celtic supporters

for a great day in the club's history. Comedian **Billy Connolly** who opened the East End stand before the game against Sporting Lisbon in August 1996.

583. He was the coolest and the most intelligent, thoughtful player I have ever seen. Willie Maley talking about right back **Alec McNair** who played for Celtic 604 times in a career that started in 1904 to 1925.

585. On 23 July 1996 Celtic beat Dutch team Reunie Borcolu 16-0 in a pre season game in Holland. The goal scorers were Cadete (6), Di Canio (4), van Hooijdonk (4), Thom and McLaughlin

586. Charlie Tully was someone special – if we went behind in a game he would always say " Don't worry lads, we always give this lot a start ", and the players around him could not help but be inspired. Celtic captain **Bertie Peacock**

587. Gordon Strachan is track suit manager who enjoys coaching, but sometimes input into tactics and coaching is less important than improving both the team morale and team spirit, and I think he must be doing a good job behind the scenes. I think if he can get every player to give their all for Celtic we will win the league again. **Pub football expert**

588. I am still trying to take it all in. There was twice the volume, twice the pace, twice the passion, of anything down in England. There is usually 10 or 15 minutes singing at a game down south, but up here it was continuous for two hours. When the crowd were singing our song Roll With It, it got to me right in the heart. Rock star **Noel Gallagher** from the Oasis band after he attended his first Old Firm game at Celtic Park in August 2000. Celtic won 6-2.

589. "I've got my eye on you." Referee to Celtic's **Peter Grant** as the teams lined up in the tunnel before an Old Firm game.

590. It was 1-1 at Celtic Park and Liverpool were heavily tipped to beat us as Anfield. We were written off. But manager Martin O'Neill really got us going before kick off in the dressing room. I can't remember a word of what he said but it was so inspirational, emotional, and brought me close to tears. I was ready for any side that night. The rest of the boys were the same. I just wish I had taped it or taken notes, as it would be great to use again. Celtic midfielder **Alan Thomson**. Celtic beat Liverpool 2-0 in the UEFA Cup at Anfield. Thomson and John Hartson scored the goals.

591. "He never scores a soft goal." Quote about **Bobby Murdoch** who scored many spectacular goals for Celtic from outside the box. His shooting power was legendary.

592. There is story that the world's greatest player Pele went into a lift in New York and after looking around he smiles and turns to one of the other passengers. " John Clark, Hampden 1966." Pele had remembered John from a 1-1 draw against Scotland. **John Clark** was a Lisbon Lion, who mastered the position of sweeper. He was nick named "the Brush" and played 318 games for Celtic.

593. Lisbon Lion Tommy **Gemmell**, scored 16 goals in season 1966-7: 4 of them in Europe. Not bad for a full back! He scored 3 against F.C. Zurich and 1 against Inter Milan.

594. " Celtic F.C. Born of Famine and Oppression." Banner at a Celtic game.

595. " I saw on the news that the fans were leaving by car and coach and that's when it really got to me that I had to be there. I would have done anything bar murder or rob a bank to see my team play in the European Cup final. But I'd just been laid off work from my job as a fireman on the old steam engines and I just couldn't raise the money to go, so I gave my scarf to a friend, John McCabe, so that if I wasn't there, at least my scarf got there." Celtic fan **Ernie Wilson** talking about Lisbon.

596. " IF SHE said "it's me or Celtic "....Would you help pack her bags? – **Pub footbal experts** dilemma on whether to go to Seville.

597. TOMMY GEMMELL ALWAYS gave off this aura of confidence before a game but, deep down, did he have any little nervous flutters? "Not usually. Maybe two or three hours before an Old Firm clash, the jitters were there but the closer it got to the game, then I felt OK. I was superstitious, though, I had to come out third in line. Even the only time I captained Celtic, against Rangers at Ibrox, I came out third with the ball!"

598. HE HAD EXCELLENCE and style and the ability to do something unexpected and unusual. He was a beacon for Celtic players to come and I want to thank the town of Ramelton for giving him to us. Celtic chairman **Brian Quinn** talking about **Patsy Gallacher** at a presentation in Ramelton county Donegal. Patsy was born in Ramelton on 16 March 1891.

599. WHEN I FIRST heard Celtic were interested in me I was surprised, not because of my background but because a club like Celtic would consider signing me. Obviously the family would have preferred that I had gone to Rangers but it was never a problem in the house and I had total support from them. Both my parents just wanted me to be what I wanted to be and despite coming from a Rangers family there was enormous respect for Celtic and Jock Stein. The Celtic fans took to me right away, though in games against Rangers I felt I had to do a bit more. I would be lying if I said otherwise and I think one or two others from the same background would tell you the same. You would never leave yourself open in an Old Firm game. If there is such a thing as another 10 per cent, then that was the match where you had to make sure you found it. You didn't want anyone to think, "He's not giving it his best shot." So you always did the full shift and more. Celtic winger **Dave Provan**.

600. JIMMY JOHNSTONE ALWAYS asked me to move to Scotland - he wanted me to play for Celtic with him. It would have been great to go there and play for Celtic but you have to remember I am from Portugal and all my family and friends were there. It would have been too difficult for me but Jimmy kept asking me anyway. Portugal legend **Eusebio.**

601. SINCE THE 1950's we had seen first the great Hungarian team, then the great Real Madrid team, then Inter Milan, then CELTIC! Yes we are credited for demonstrating that defensive football was not the route that football should take. Playing football The Celtic Way is credited with demonstrating that the Italian defensive system of Catannachio was limited. Playing football the Celtic way means playing with panache, passion and being gallus. In summary entertaining the fans. **Harry Brady**

602. CELTIC RESERVES WERE due to play Scotland in a practice game at Lesser Hampden. Jock Stein came into the boot room before the game and told me he was making me captain of Celtic for that game. " **It is for the future**" he explained. I knew he thought a lot of me, but this was a great surprise. But also great pressure. **George Connelly**.

603. JOCK STEIN KNEW which players he could give a verbal telling off and which players needed to be coaxed. If he had bawled me out when I was a youngster I know I could not have taken it. I remember one day he gave senior players Billy McNeill and Jimmy Johnstone a tongue lashing. I made up my mind that day that I was going to be well behaved. **Danny McGrain**

604. HE IS A very honest man. He is honest in his assessments of the quality of the team, and that includes both collectively and individually. He is honest with the players, but he is also very human in his understanding because as a former player he knows

what they are going through. **Dermot Desmond**, Celtic's major shareholder, talking about manager Martin O'Neill.

605. "I REMEMBER WHEN I became a team-mate, I had never seen a man so content with his life. Playing for Celtic in their centenary year then returning to his family." Ex Celtiic player **Billy Stark** talking about his friend Tommy Burns at his funeral service in St.Marys in the Calton on 21 May 2008. Tommy was devoted to his wife, Rosemary, and his four children, and his grandson, Cole.

606. WE ARE NOT a great team, but we are a team of great promise. There will be no let up in our efforts to become a great team. We must go all out to make Celtic again one of the great names in the world of football. We want to give the supporters a team to be proud of. We also want to be proud of our supporters, not just the vast majority of them, but every single one of them. With the proper encouragement Celtic can go forward to great things. **Jock Stein** writing in issue number 1 of The Celtic View on 11 August 1965.

607. I REMEMBER THE first time I saw young Peter. He was about 16 years old and playing in a cup final for the Celtic Boys Club. How could I forget that wee guy that stood in the centre circle pointing that everything that moved? And as for those haircuts ? He has been everything from Little Lord Fauntleroy to Mike Flowers – his wife likes experimenting on him. Tommy Burns talking his friend and team mate **Peter Grant**.

608. MY MOTHER GAVE our close a good scrub, the highest mark of respect a Glaswegian can give a guest, the night that Sean Fallon came to our house in Drumchapel to discuss me joining Celtic. She even gave him a personal escort to our flat on the top landing in case he did not make it up the stairs. **Danny McGrain**

609. To PLAY ALONGSIDE Patsy Gallacher in the Cup Final was a dream. Patsy was the fastest man over 10 yards. He moved at great speed and could stop immediately sending opponents in all directions. He could win a game when the rest of us were just thinking about it. **Jimmy McGrory**

610. I WATCHED ENDLESS videos of Pele in action when I was growing up. Everything about him has already been said: he had unbelievable skill and control. There is little doubt Pele was the greatest player of all time. **Henrik Larsson.**

611. " IF YOU care about your club turn up at the City Halls in Glasgow's Candleriggs tomorrow night." **Matt McGlone** paid £95 to put this advert in a Sunday paper in September 1993. He was one of the five men who formed the Celts for Change fans movement, which stopped the club going into receivership. Thirty six people turned up for the first meeting. Three hundred and sixty fans turned up for the meeting on the second week. Eventually approx two thousand fans attended the meetings.

612. " SAY JIMMY that it is not true, that you must quit the game. For we are oh so proud of you, and glory in your fame. Your name is known from Pole to Pole, full many an exile sighs, the idol of all Celtic hearts, Jimmy Quinn from Croy." Poem in Glasgow Observer newspaper in August 1914 with the impending retirement of **Jimmy Quinn**

613. IF ANYONE HITS you, don't let them see that you are hurt. Just get up as if nothing has happened. **Sean Fallon** used to say to the young players. Sean was known as The Iron Man and just got on with the game.

614. WHEN I WAS four years old I was the mascot on the St.Andrew's Brake Club and I well remember being pulled along on a horse drawn wagon to watch the Celts. Our base was in George Street near George Square and all our members came from the surround-

ing area. **James Flaherty** speaking in 1994. He had been watching Celtic for the past 74 years.

615. NEIL MOCHAN SIGNED for Celtic in 1953. He played 268 games and scored 111 goals. On 29 February 1960 he scored all 5 goals when Celtic beat St.Mirren in a Scottish Cup replay. He was the trainer of the Lisbon Lions. There is a famous picture of him jumping off the bench at the end of the European Cup Final in Lisbon to celebrate victory with a huge smile on his face. He loved Celtic and gave a lifetime of service to the club.

616. I WON'T BE expecting a pay rise or anything like that, if I do well. Everything is quite clear in the contract, so there is no problem. **Henrik Larsson** at the press conference on the day he signed for Celtic making it clear he would honour his contract.

617. I KEEP GETTING reminded that I never scored against Rangers in a Celtic jersey, but my answer to that was I didn't need to. **Joe McBride**

618. WILLIE MALEY WAS like a headmaster at school. But I soon learned to fight my corner. When he signed me he promised me four pounds a week as soon as I got into the first team. After my first game, I played a few more times that season, but I never got my money. The older players said I would have to go to his office and argue my case. I did and got my four pounds. **Willie Buchan** who played 134 games between 1933 and 1937

619. LISBON LION **BOBBY Murdoch** had a cameo role in the TV movie "Down among the Big Boys.". He plays a man drinking in bar when the main character Jo Jo (Billy Connolly) comes in for a pint. In real life Billy Connolly is a huge Celtic fan. The film was a thriller/crime with plenty of comedy moments.

620. ARE YOU GOING to Dublin for the St.Patrick's Day celebrations? " Wee man, I am staying here in Rutherglen. When you are a Celtic

supporter every day is St.Patricks' Day". **The pub football expert**

621. JOCK STEIN LIKED to get involved but his bad ankle meant that he couldn't run much, so sometimes he took it out on his goalkeepers. **Ronnie Simpson.** Jock disliked goalkeepers because one of their mistakes could wreck all his plans.

622. " IN YOU go wee man", Jock Stein pointed to the dressing room as **Danny McGrain** took cramp. This was Danny's first ever pre season training session with the Celtic first team, including the Lisbon Lions. He had just joined Celtic and it was the first time big Jock watched him in training. Danny knocked over every hurdle he was trying to jump because of the cramp! What a first impression. Pre season training is tough even for experienced professionals and Jock wanted to look after his young player.

623. IN 1967 THE Argentine Press claimed that the only way to stop **El Chico** (their nick name for Jimmy Johnstone) in the World Club Championship against Racing Club, was to shoot him. They booted Jimmy black and blue in all three games. He later said that Juan Carlos Rulli was the toughest player he ever played against.

624. I REMEMBER OUR brake club travelling back into Glasgow when we beat Rangers 5-0 in the semi final of the Scottish Cup in 1925. When we reached Glasgow Cross a policeman raised one hand to stop the horse and someone from our club shouted: " It is alright officer, we were at the game, we already know the score." **Davie Collins** aged 93.

625. THERE IS A wonderful picture of **Jock Stein** near the end of the European Cup Final in Lisbon. With only a few minutes to play, he quietly got off his seat at the side of the field, and walked up the track towards the dressing room. He left his staff on the touchline bench, Neil Mochan, Bob Rooney, Jimmy Steel, Sean Fallon, and substitute John Fallon, to enjoy the victory with all the players.

Jock waited in the dressing room to celebrate with his players. He did not want to divert attention away from his players.

626. CELTIC MANAGER **GORDON Strachan** started off his career as a player with Dundee. **Jimmy Johnstone** also played with Dundee at that time and he was coming to the end of his football career. They made up " one of the smallest midfields in the history of Dundee Football Club". Jinky was a huge hero to Gordon Strachan

627. " YOU CAN take us anywhere and we won't let you down". This is a line from the song Over and Over, and describes the Celtic supporters.

628. I LIKE TALKING, annoying the other players in the dressing room in the morning, slagging their gear, and hearing that Rangers have lost. Celtic midfielder **Peter Grant**

629. A FEW WEEKS before the European Cup Final in 1970, Tommy Gemmell was involved in a car crash. His car mounted a grass verge, struck a signpost and overturned near his home in Kirkintilloch. A passing motorist administered first aid after Tommyl crawled out from under the wreckage. A doctor put 3 stitches into a wound in his head. Celtic's physiotherapist Jimmy Steel stayed at Gemmell's home that night to give him treatment for a thigh injury he picked up in the crash. **www.stateofthegame.co.uk**

630. **JIMMY QUINN** PLAYED for Celtic between 1963-1974. He is considered to be one of the quickest players ever to play for Celtic. When he retired he was working on a building site and one day a young boy about 20 years old challenged him to race around the building site at lunch time. Jimmy was around forty years old. The young fella had brought his running shoes. Jimmy put down his cheese sandwich, and was still wearing his working boots. Jimmy left the young fella a long way behind in their race! Jimmy Quinn died when he was in his early fifties.

631. **PADDY CONNOLLY** WAS an outside right and played for Celtic between 1921-1932. He was nicknamed The Greyhound because he was very quick. He was also reckoned to be one of the best crosser of a football in the Celtic history. Paddy played almost 300 times for Celtic.

632. WHEN **MARTIN O'NEILL** joined Celtic as manager he learned very quickly the types of questions he can expect from journalists at press conferences. At his first meeting he was asked by a journalist " If you can't beat Rangers will you leave?" Martin looked over his specs and replied, " Well, night follows day doesn't it, and do we play them next week?" He understood quickly a wrong answer to a trivial question could be on the back page of some papers for days.

633. IN SEASON 1947/48 we travelled to Dundee and we were in danger of being relegated for the first time ever. We got to Dundee the night before the match, and chairman Bob Kelly told us to go out and relax. So we went out and had a beer or two and then went to bed. **John McPhail**. Celtic won the match 3-2.

634. "REVIE'S SHITTING HIMSELF. I've never seen that man as nervous in all my life. He's as white as a sheet. If he is like that, what do you think his players are like? They are there for the taking, believe you me." **Jock Stein** to his players before the European Cup semi final against Leeds United in 1970. Don Revie was the Leeds manager

635. MY BEST CELTIC memory was listening to the radio when Celtic won the European Cup. I was at a convention in Montreal in Canada. I had a short wave radio picking up the BBC World Service. **Fergus McCann**

636. FOOTBALL IS CHANGING. Full back used to be the least glamorous job on the park. They were expected to do only two things, scare wingers and belt the ball up the park. Dunky Mackay who

played with me at Celtic in the early 1960's always had ideas about overlapping and joining in the attack: he was ahead of his time. My own position at centre half was to stop goals being scored, not to get you name on the score sheet. But that all changed in 1961. We were playing Ayr United at Somerset Park and we were losing 1-0 at half time. I remember sitting with Paddy Crerand and Bertie Peacock and saying that I was going to nip up field if I got the opportunity. I did and I scored and we won 3-1. When Jock Stein became manager it became a regular tactic for me to go up for corner kicks. **Billy McNeill**

637. WHEN I STARTED my career with Stenhousemuir I was an old fashioned outside right with sawdust on my boots. When I moved from Hearts to Celtic I shuffled around inside right, centre, and inside left. I was told later that one Hearts official said I could be transferred because he thought I would be no use to Celtic! Lisbon Lion **Willie Wallace.**

638. THE FIRST 25 entrants to the Celtic Hall of Fame were announced at a dinner in Glasgow on Saturday 22 September 2001. Pat Bonner, Tom Boyd, Tommy Burns, Steve Chalmers, John Clark, Bobby Collins, Dixie Deans, Sean Fallon, Patsy Gallacher, David Hay, Paul Lambert, Jimmy Johnstone, Joe McBride, Danny McGrain, Jimmy McGrory, Mudo MacLeod, Billy McNeill, Billy McPhail, Paul McStay, Neil Mochan, Lubo Moravcik, Ronnie Simpson, Johnny Thomson, Charlie Tully and Willie Wallace. Brian Scott won the Cardinal Winning Lifetime Achievement Award, the New York CSC won the Bobby Murdoch Award, and a special award was made to Jock Stein

639. " THERE ARE not many statues built to critics. To achieve what we have achieved, not just domestically but in Europe, is a testimony to the whole club, but particularly to the manager Gordon Strachan and the players." Celtic chairman **John Reid's** answer to

people who knock the Celtic manager Gordon Strachan who had delivered 3 league titles in 3 seasons.

640. I AM NOT here to be popular, I am here to win football matches. **Gordon Strachan**.

641. I'D LOVE TO have been a rally driver. I think it would be a really exciting lifestyle. But in reality though, without blowing my own trumpet too much, I'm brainy enough to have gone to university, studied for a mathematics degree, and be a teacher. Celtic centre half **Tony Mowray** when asked what job he would liked to have done if he had not made it as a footballer.

642. " THE GREATEST honour of my life", new Celtic chairman **John Reid** describes his appointment in September 2007

643. FERGUS McCANN WAS great hero of mine. Without him we would still have the biscuit tin. Fergus did everything he said he would do. His work stands silently in his praise now that he has left Celtic. **Billy Connolly**.

644. **BOBBY MURDOCH** WAS a hard player with visionary passing and a lethal shot. His tackling nullified opponents – ask the Rangers players of the time, they called him Bobby Murder.

645. **BERTIE PEACOCK** WAS nick named " The Little Ant" due to his work rate and ability to get around the football park. He played 453 games for Celtic and was part of the team that beat Rangers 7-1. There is bronze statue of Bertie in his home town of Coleraine in Northern Ireland. There is a plaque on it inscribed, " Sportsman, Statesman, and Gentleman".

646. WITHOUT QUESTION, SOME of our players are phenomenally fit. Scott Brown's engine is something I've never seen before: the guy was still jumping up and down at 11o'clock last night - he's like one of those Duracell battery bunnies. **Scott McDonald** after Celtic beat Rangers 2-0 in the 2009 League Cup Final after extra

time. The head of Celtic's sport science department, Frenchman Gregory Dupont, is in charge of the Celtic players fitness program. " He does a lot of power work and concentrates on biometric exercises, which nobody had done before. It is short, sharp stuff. We do power runs but nothing long distance: everything is explosive."

647. THERE IS NOTHING worse than players who don't enjoy playing. I hate it when you can tell that a player is just going through the motions. They should love the game and be proud to play it. **Charlie Nicholas**

648. **ALEC BENNETT** WON four league championship winner medals with Celtic. He was part of the great forward line Bennett, McMenemy, Quinn, Somers, Hamilton. He later joined Rangers and won three league championship winner medals.

649. THE CELTIC PLAYERS used to call the period in the early 1960's when Celtic did not win any trophies the B.S. period (Before Stein)

650. THE MCSTAY BROTHERS (Jimmy and Willie McStay) played in the 1925 Scottish Cup win over Dundee. In 1985 the McStay brothers (Paul and Willie) played in the Scottish Cup win over Dundee United.

651. IN MARCH, 1994 Fergus McCann joined the club and for the first time in its history Celtic was made a PLC and with it bought the most successful share issue of any football club in the world. The Celtic supporters were given the chance to own a piece of their history. "Celtic Four Reasons Why You Should Become a Shareholder" was the name of the brochure that was issued explaining the benefits of being a shareholder and the cost. By investing £620 a supported would receive one unit of five ordinary shares. The brochure cover had some great photographs of the first

ever Celtic team, the Lisbon Lions, Tommy Burns, Paul McStay, and Jock Stein as a player.

652. " IN THE war against Rangers in the fight for the cup, **Jimmy McGrory** put the Celtic one up. He's done it before and he'll do it again, Oh Jimmy McGrory, The Pride of Parkhead." A song that used to echo around Celtic Park

653. WHEN CELTIC WERE preparing for away games in Europe in the 1960's Jock Stein used to gather the players around the blackboard and discuss tactics. **Jimmy Johnstone** spent much of the time cleaning his nails or looking out the window. Jock would then ask the players if they had any questions. Jimmy always angered big Jock by asking him how long the flight would be! Jinky was not scared of any opponent, but he was scared of flying in an aeroplane.

654. CHARLIE TULLY WAS a character. He did not look like an athlete, but make no mistake, he could play like one. He had a superb footballing brain and could mesmerise players and defences alike. **Sean Fallon** talking about his team mate Charles Patrick Tully

655. MY CELTIC PRIDE, I will not hide, my Celtic race, I will not disgrace, my Celtic blood, flows hot and true, My Celtic people, I will stand by you, through thick and thin, till the day we die, our Celtic flag, always stands so high shout this poem louder than all the rest, cos everyone knows, we Hoops are the best. **Robert Taylor**

656. CELTIC's **BOBO BALDE** bought 100 Celtic tops in Scotland for fans in Africa. He wanted Celtic to have lots of fans in his native Guinea. They wore them at the African Nations Cup finals, and the colourful Celtic jersey was splashed on TV screens across the African continent.

657. MY DAD ALWAYS told me to stay on the level all the time: not get to high or to down. But this is what playing for Celtic does to you. But to come here to Liverpool and perform like that as a team is just brilliant. **John Hartson**.

658. I HAD GIVEN the team no special instructions before the game, except to play fairly and not be goaded into retaliation. Celtic manager **Jimmy McGrory** before the 7-1 victory over Rangers in 1957

659. HE WAS HAILED as " Celtic's new Jock Stein." A Sports journalist description of **Billy McNeill** in a Glasgow evening paper after his first appearance in the league team against Clyde in August 1958.

660. THE SADDEST GAME I have ever seen was the day the great John Thomson died after a game against Rangers at Ibrox in 1931. My abiding memory is of the Rangers captain Davie Meiklejohn going behind the goal and raising his arms to stop the Rangers fans shouting abuse as John lay on the ground injured. Since then I formed a great friendship with John's brother, and through that I received Johns bible. If I had kept the bible it would only be sitting in a drawer, so I presented it to Celtic and it is now on permanent view in the stadium. **James Flaherty** speaking in 1994. He had been watching Celtic for the past 74 years.

661. I SCORED ONE of my best goals in May 1979 when we beat Rangers 4-2 at Celtic Park to win the league. Tommy Burns was not playing that night but I remember him in his shirt and tie standing on the wall beside the Directors Box giving it laldy. **George McCluskey**

662. I REMEMBER THE horse drawn fire brigade carriages coming along London Road when the stadium went on fire in 1904. All the neighbours watched the firemen fight in vain to save the stand in Janefield Street, which was replaced the following year by the cov-

ered enclosure (that we used to know as the Jungle). **Dr.Thomas McKail** who was born in 1897 and lived in London Road.

663. I WAS SUPERSTITIOUS as a player, and stick to my routine. I always sit on the sixth seat on the bus and always sit next to Tommy Gemmell. I always run out to the park as the fifth player. John Clark is in front of me, and Bobby Lennox behind me. Billy McNeill always wanders around the dressing room with only his jersey and underpants on until we get the referees signal to go onto the park.! Big Tommy Gemmell always runs out and hits the ball into the net before every game. **Bertie Auld**

664. AIDEN MCGEADY'S IMPROVEMENT as a player is undoubtedly down to Gordon Strachan. When he was a young boy he was much better than other lads and when he stepped up into the real world it took him a bit of time to adapt because it was harder for him and he couldn't just easily skip past players the way he used to, but his manager has helped him develop. Ireland Under-21 manager, **Don Givens**

665. ENRICO ANNONI'S STRENGTH is that he defends his goal. He is a real defender. **Tommy Burns** after signing the tough Italian. Rico was a specialist at man marking

666. I HAD THREE daughters. My eldest liked football and her favourite players were Derek Whyte and Alan McInally. My middle daughter had no interest – she was watching TV one day when we were playing Rangers and asked what colour of strip I had on ! My youngest used to ask me every day when I got home from training if Celtic had won. **Danny McGrain**

667. IN 1961 CELTIC lost in the Scottish Cup final to Dunfermline, who were managed by **Jock Stein**. Soon after this game Jock attended a seminar in England to hear the football thoughts of Gustav Sebes. He was the coach behind the great Hungarian team of the early 1950s who played a form of attacking football that

destroyed most other teams, including a 6-3 victory over England at Wembley. Sebes was a always looking to invent new ways of playing attacking football, rather than just spoiling games. He pioneered the 4-2-4 system. He also advocated what he referred to as " *Socialist Football* ", which was an early version of Total Football with every player pulling equal weight and able to play in all positions on the pitch. Jock was always looking for ways to improve his football knowledge, and the Hungarian way of playing football made a big impression on him.

668. **BOBBY EVANS** WAS a relaxed character. He used to read comics in the dressing room. At half time during big games he would jump onto the massage table and go for a sleep! He was a great player for Celtic and played between 1944 until 1960

669. THE FIRST CELTIC Park had nine gates around the ground for spectators to gain entrance.

670. I WAS ALWAYS tall – I ate more potatoes than anyone else in our house, and like all the Irish, we are a very big family. **Pat Bonner,** who played 607 games in goal for Celtic.

671. How CAN I forget when bandits like you keep reminding me ? **Willie Maley** to a customer in his restaurant (The Bank in Queen Street) who asked him if he could remember the game that Motherwell beat Celtic 8-0. This match was played on a Friday night in April 1937. All the Celtic player were travelling down to London later that night to watch the English FA Cup Final on the Saturday. The previous week Celtic had won the Scottish Cup. Some of the players were not in the best of condition for the Motherwell game.

672. " I AM a great believer in coincidences. Shay's (Given) is the best keeper to come out of Ireland since Packie Bonnar, and they are both from Donegal". Celtic manager **Liam Brady** taking about

goalkeeper Shay Given who signed for Celtic in 1992 aged sixteen.

673. I PLAYED HARD and I respected opponents who did the same. I believe that tackling is part and parcel of the game, and it can be as much an art as any other part of football. **Sean Fallon**, Celtic's Iron Man in the 1950's. Sean became assistant manager to the great Jock Stein.

674. **ROY AITKEN** PLAYED his first game for Celtic in 1975 when he was still at school in Ayrshire. If Celtic were preparing for a European game at their favourite retreat in Seamill Hydro, he joined his team mates after school, stayed overnight, then caught a bus back to school in the morning.

675. ON 25 FEBRUARY 1922 Celtic were playing Hamilton Academicals at Celtic Park in the Scottish Cup. Celtic were losing 3-0 at half time in a dreadful performance. Manager **Willie Maley** kept the players on the park at half time and gave them a rollicking in front of the huge crowd. The final score was 3-1 to Hamilton.

676. I NEVER REGRETTED turning down a move to Manchester United when I was 17 years old to join Celtic. It was fantastic for me. My heroes were Willie Fernie, Bobby Collins and Charlie Tully and now I was playing beside these guys just a few years after I was pretending to be them in playground matches. **Mike Jackson** who scored 32 goals in 78 games between 1957 and 1963. He left Celtic for St.Johnstone a few years before Jock Stein became manager, and a lot of his team mates and friends went onto become Lisbon Lions.

677. WHEN I SIGNED for Celtic the job I was given by the manager, Jock Stein, was very simple. He told me I was employed to prevent stupid goals. During that season I hardly ever crossed over the halfway line. **Pat Stanton** who signed for Celtic in 1976 from Hibs.

678. **JOHN THOMSON**, CELTIC's great young goalkeeper, was short and stocky - he was about five feet nine inches tall. He had extraordinary strength in his hands. Sometimes in training he would prove his strength by holding a moderately hard shot with only a finger of each hand. **Angus MacVicar**, writer

679. HE COULD JUMP like a cat. Steve Callaghan the Celtic scout who signed **John Thomson**. He also signed Jimmy McGrory.

680. THAT'S THE STUFF, just you give it right back to me. It is good for the team if we shout at each other. **Patsy Gallacher** to his team mate Jimmy McStay. Patsy was not slow to tell other players if they were not performing to a high level. Jimmy got fed up after one moan, and shouted back at the star man. Patsy to his credit took it on the chin.

681. SEASON 1966/1967 WAS probably the greatest season in Celtic's history. They won 5 trophies including the European Cup. The season started when Celtic played Rangers at Ibrox on 02 August 1966 in the Glasgow Cup. This competition attracted massive crowds in the 1960's as the six Glasgow teams battled for the trophy. There was 76,000 people at Ibrox to watch Celtic win 4-0. Bobby Lennox scored three goals, and Billy McNeill scored the other goal with a left foot shot. The Celtic team bus was late at arriving because the driver took the wrong road to Ibrox. The Celtic players quickly got changed and started the season in style. This gave them confidence for a fantastic season.

682. EVERY TIME I walk in the front door at Celtic Park, I still feel an immense pride, and at the same time an immense humility because of the way the fans respond to all of the Lisbon Lions. **Bertie Auld**

683. IN 1924 CELTIC played a friendly against Third Lanark. It was an unusual game as two referees were used as an experiment. It was not a great success, and it never happened again.

684. It is murder going for a drink with Packie Bonnar, because he's got short arms and long pockets. He is a great goalkeeper but how does he do it with those short arms. Celtic defender **Mark McNally** jokes about his team mate.

685. One of my low points of my time at Celtic was when Fergus McCann was booed onto the filed to unfurl the league flag. Ex Celtic chairman **Brian Quinn**. He was amazed that some supporters never recognised the contribution of Fergus to Celtic.

686. When we beat Rangers 7-1 I wouldn't say it was the highlight of my Celtic career. My favourite was when we beat Rangers 3-2 in the Glasgow Charity Cup Final in 1950. It was a carnival occasion with Hollywood star Danny Kaye at the game. I was still a rookie player and to be on the same field as some of the great Celtic players was a thrill. **Bertie Peacock** who was captain of the 7-1 team.

687. In 1966 Celtic were in Tbilisi to play Dynamo Kiev. A number of supporters were staying in the same hotel as the Celtic players, but the food was terrible. Celtic had brought their own food and chef, so they shared all their food with the fans. It is not often you get Jimmy Johnstone dropping a chicken leg onto your plate.

688. I could have been the first attacking, over lapping goalkeeper. Lisbon Lion **Tommy Gemmell**. In the day before substitutes were allowed, Tommy went in goal if the Celtic keeper was injured. He did in five times in all, three times with the first team and twice with the reserves. He never lost a goal !

689. Celtic played in the testimonial game for England's World Cup winning captain Bobby Moore. The match was played on November 16th 1970: the attendance at Upton Park (West Ham United) was 24,448 and the score was 3-3. A match programme autographed by Bobby Moore, Jock Stein, Billy McNeil, Bobby

Lennox, Harry Hood, Jimmy Johnston, later sold at Christie's auctions for £583.

690. "SCORE AN EARLY goal and press on regardless boys." A quote from Celtic and Scotland masseur, **Jimmy Steele**. He was a great friend of Jock Stein. He would often say this to players before a game.

691. BOBBY MURDOCH GAME me my first team chance when he was manager at Middlesbrough. I will forever be grateful to him for that opportunity. **Tony Mowbray**

692. "PLAY LIKE BLAZES till you score, then take it easy. They can't drop you if you score. " **Gerald Padua McAloon**. He played as a forward for Celtic in the 1940's. Celtic manager Jimmy McGrory wanted to exchange him for a Belfast Celtic player called Charlie Tully, but the deal fell through.

693. FIRST AND FOREMOST, Du Wei is here as a footballer, who manager Gordon Strachan feels has great potential. We have reached saturation point commercially in Scotland and Ireland, which are our core markets, and we have to look at other areas. The Chinese market is potentially even more lucrative than the Japanese one. **Peter Lawwell**, Celtic Chief Executive, after signing 23 year old Chinese centre half Du Wei.

694. WE ARE WORKING to develop a Chinese website. We will use it to sell appropriate merchandising to the Chinese market. Our popular 'Channel 67' service will provide subscribers with broadband content; we'll be able to broadcast matches live over the internet and so on. If all goes according to plan, the club's green and white stripes will soon be seen on Shanghai streets, assuming, of course, the pirates don't beat us to it. Commercial director **David Thomson**

695. WHAT I REMEMBER about the night we played Leeds United at Hampden in the semi final of the European Cup was walking

out of the tunnel and feeling like we were playing in a dome. We couldn't see the floodlights because there were so many people there and their breath in the cold night air blocked out the floodlights. **Bertie Auld.**

696. CELTIC PARK WAS used as a venue for different sports in the early years. There was a cycle and running track around the pitch. Manager **Willie Maley** was interested in various sports including athletics. In 1897 nearly 50,000 people watched the World Cycling Championship. In 1918 almost 12,000 fans attended a baseball game! Hurling was also played. In 1937 World Champion boxer Benny Lynch from the Gorbals fought Jim Warnock, but lost this non title fight on points. 20,000 people attended the fight.

697. " HE'S GOT no hair we don't care, walking in a Hartson wonderland ". Song that was belted out at Celtic Park when **John Hartson** scored a goal

698. CELTIC GOALKEEPER **RONNIE Simpson** had amazing concentration. He would prowl across his goal line with his eyes glued to the far end of the park 100 yards away with Celtic attacking the other end.

699. "SAVE TOMMY. SAVE **Tommy McInally**" shouted the old Irish fella to the fireman who was called to deal with a flood in his tenement. The fireman rushed into the bedroom and found a picture of Celtic's **Tommy McInally** above his bed.

700. " WHEN BOBBY Murdoch is fully fit". **Jock Stein's** response to a question when asked if Celtic would win the European Cup again

701. " To HELP put Rangers back in their place." Quote attributed to **Chris Sutton** on the day he signed for Celtic.

702. "JUST CALL me lucky Danny." **Danny McGrain** overcame some serious injuries in his career including a fractured skull, diabetes,

and a traumatic ankle injury. World class is a term often used to describe players, and Danny was a truly world class footballer.

703. " Malcolm, son, if I have the ball and you want it just shout for it and I'll pass, but make sure it is the right shout." **Malcolm McDonald** remembers the advice he got from a senior player before he played his first game for Celtic against Partick Thistle in 1932. He was still at school and played at outside left in this game. Malky became a Celtic great and served the club between 1932 and 1945. He scored a hat trick in the 6-2 win over Rangers in September 1938.

704. " Tonight Mr Stein people know how good a team you are: you've proved how good you are." BBC Sports commentator David Coleman to **Jock Stein** after Celtic beat Leeds United in the semi final of the European Cup." No" replied Jock. " We didn't need to show how good this Celtic team is. You ask Shankly or Matt Busby, these men knew we were a good team. Only English commentators didn't realise how good a team we were. People who know about football knew we were a good team"

705. Back in the early days the physios had a few unusual ways of treating injuries. For example, if you had a bad ankle you could find yourself standing naked under the shower getting a cold hose aimed at your ankle. They did a lot of different things, even going out and trying to block the ball on your injured side, things you would never do now. Football has changed and it's changed for the better in that respect. You just didn't want to be injured anyway, because if you were injured you were out the team and didn't get your bonuses and you still had the mortgage to pay. You tried to get fit as quickly as you could. **Bobby Lennox**, who scored goals for Celtic across 3 decades, the 1960s, '70s and '80s.

706. I live my life day to day now and don't ask myself too many questions. I changed after the death of my friend and team mate

David Di Tommaso   His death made me think deeply about lots of things. Now I don't live for the future, I live for the moment. **Marc-Antoine Fortune**

707. APART FROM ME and Jinky, we had a few guys who fancied themselves as the best singer. I always liked to hear Bertie Auld sing. He is a great chanter, while big Tam Gemmell would sing 'From Russia with Love'. Jock Stein sometimes handed the microphone around the bus on long trips and everyone had to do a song. **Bobby Lennox.**

708. " IT WAS one of those shots I knew was a goal as soon as I hit it." **Joe Mclaughlin**. He burst the net at Celtic Park with a ferocious shot. (against Third Lanark I think in April 1945). Joe was Celtic's captain during season 1944-45. He is one of the few Celtic defenders to have scored an own goal against Rangers.

709. THE BEST DEFENSIVE systems, especially drilled ones, can be beaten with players who have flair and imagination. Here at Celtic we have those players. **Jock Stein**

710. AT SCHOOL, ST.MICHAEL's, they only played Gaelic football. The nuns threatened to expel me because I was playing football on a Saturday rather than playing for the school Gaelic team. My Dad had to go up and see the head nun and sort a few things out. **Neil Lennon**. He left school at 16 years old with seven "O" levels.

711. IN APRIL 1947 Celtic had to travel to Dundee in their last league game of the season. Celtic had to win to avoid the danger of relegation. With 30 minutes to play Dundee were winning 2-1. **Jock Weir** scored the winner for Celtic in the 88th minute to win 3-2. He wrote himself into the Celtic history book with his hat trick in that game.

712. I AM TELLING you wee man, I had the Shingles, but that wee physio up the Gallowgate cured me. He had just touched a pair of boots

that belonged to Henrik Larsson after he scored that great goal in the 6-2 against Rangers. It was a miracle. **Pub football expert**

713. One player who sticks in my mind is the little red haired winger **Jimmy Johnstone**. He had such skill and was the kind of player I always enjoy watching. Pele, the worlds greatest ever footballer talking about Jinky

714. **Henrik Larsson** met his hero, Pele, at a presentation at Euro 1996. " It was a great moment for me. He had this aura about him. I opened my mouth to speak but nonsense just came out !" said Henrik.

715. Disappointments can sometimes be more significant that victories. They make the players see that whatever we are going to do here, we have to do it ourselves. I do not like having a go at players, but sometimes it is important to show the players that the time for excuses is over. **Billy McNeill**

716. I am not trying to look like Jimmy Johnstone, or draw attention to myself. In fact in some ways I have regrets about it, because Celtic have such a tradition for their players being well turned out. Winger **Davie Provan** after he joined Celtic from Kilmarnock. His trademark was his socks rolled down to his ankles when he played.

717. **Jimmy McGrory** was a Celtic player for 15 years, and it was said that he only ever had four pairs of football boots, because he headed the ball more in a game that he kicked it! In those days footballs were made of leather or pigskin and in wet weather the ball got heavier as the game progressed. It took some courage to head a ball, but Jimmy scored hundreds of goals with his head. But his greatest legacy was the spirit in which he played football. In an era when forwards were fouled often and got rough tackling, he never retaliated. Jimmy was a gentleman and will never be forgotten by the Celtic fans.

718. " WE ARE Celtic supporters, Different drinks, Different Feelings, but the same colours " . Swedish Celtic supporters website.

719. IT WASN'T THE most stylish goal you ever saw, Tommy Coyne got a touch from a corner and the ball dropped to me. I hooked it towards goal and it trickled past the Rangers keeper Chris Woods. But the feeling could not have been any better if I'd rattled it in from thirty yards. I just went daft celebrating. **Anton Rogan**, who played left back in the 1988 Centenary Team that won the league.

720. HE WAS ONE of the greatest Celtic players. **Sunny Jim Young** played between 1903 and 1917. He won 10 league championship winners medals. (1905-1910, and 1914-1917). In 1904 he was playing against Third Lanark and whacked the referee in the face with the ball while he was clearing it up field. The ball hit the whistle, and the referee lost five of his teeth.

721. " ARMS HELD high, spread out like ostrich wings, head down, back slightly bent forward, enormous feet". Newspaper description of Celtic's first great goal scorer **Sandy McMahon**

722. WITHOUT FANS WHO pay at the turnstile, football is nothing. Sometimes we are inclined to forget that. The only chance of bringing them into stadiums is if they are entertained by what happens on the football field. **Jock Stein**

723. BEFORE I JOINED Celtic I had played under 13 different managers at other clubs. The team talks ranged from " Do you not want your bonus ? to " All the best lads have a good game". But under Jock Stein it was different. He told you what you had to do and why. **Harry Hood**.

724. ONE OF THE must stunning trophies in the Celtic trophy room is the Ferencvaros Vase. This was put up by the Budapest Club in 1914 for a charity competition between Celtic and Burnley, which

was played in Hungary. The game ended in a draw and could not be replayed as Celtic were returning to Scotland the next day. The game was replayed in Burnley and Celtic won 2-0, but the cup never arrived! In 1988 on the day Celtic won the Centenary League Championship at Celtic Park when they beat Dundee, the Ferencvaros officials had flew into Glasgow and presented Celtic with this magnificent trophy to set matters right from 1914. What a wonderful gesture.

725. " HERE'S THE ball – it is like you full of wind". Celtic's **George Paterson** to referee Mr.Dale, after he awarded Rangers a soft penalty in the semi final of the Victory Cup at Hampden in 1946. George was usually a player who accepted referees decisions but the referee had made some erratic decisions during the game. George was sent off for the first time in his career. At half time George had reported the smell of drink on the refs breath. Celtic's Jimmy Mallan was also sent off at the penalty incident after he rubbed out the penalty spot with the sole of his boot.

726. ONE OF THE best decisions in the clubs history was in 1895 when the Celtic committee refused to pass a suggestion that they should restrict the number of Protestant players to three signings. In fact the policy was that Celtic could sign as many Protestants as they wanted. Across the city Rangers had a different policy. It was only when FIFA started to hint that they were going to have a close look at the Rangers policy in the 1980's that they had to change for commercial reasons. It was incredible how the media in Scotland ignored Rangers attitude during the last century.

727. I AM THE sort of player who can be out the game for 85 minutes before scoring. But those 85 minutes were not spent idly watching. It is up to me to seek out scoring opportunities throughout the game, and then put them into action when the opportunity arises. I won't worry about expectations, after all it is only football. **Harald Brattbakk** signed for Celtic from Norwegian team

Rosenberg, where he scored 127 goals in 148 games. Harald now works as an airline pilot in Norway.

728. "I FELT FULL of confidence. But when I started to walk out of the centre circle towards the penalty area, the tension hit me. I asked Jimmy Johnstone to say a quick prayer for me, and I then said another quietly to myself." **Dixie Deans** talking about his famous penalty miss in the semi final of the European Cup against Inter Milan at Celtic Park. He ballooned his kick over the bar and Celtic lost 5-4.

729. I REALISE JUST how important the fans are to Celtic, and sometimes I reckon the tension during a match is worse for them than for the players. I know of fans who left Celtic Park, including my own brother, before the penalty shoot out with Inter Milan in the European Cup semi final. **Bobby Murdoch**

730. I WAS IN awe of Danny McGrain when we started to play in the same team together. I couldn't bring myself to call Danny by his first name! He was the best in the world in his position and yet never so big time that he could not spare a moment to give a teenager the benefit of his experience. **Peter Grant** talking about Danny McGrain

731. MOTHERWELL, IBROX, DUNFERMLINE, Kilmarnock, Tynecastle, Hampden, Bayview, Easter Road, Brockville. Celtic won their nine-in-a-row championships on nine different grounds. They won at Hampden, because Celtic Park was under reconstruction that season. Rangers finished runner up 6 times, Aberdeen twice, and Hibs once.

732. **FRANK McAVENNIE** USED to fly down to London after a Celtic game on a Saturday night to spend the weekend with his model girlfriend. He was always late for training on the Monday morning, and manager Billy McNeill used to fine him. One Monday morning Frank flew up on the early flight, hired the Radio Clyde

" eye in the sky" helicopter ,and landed at the Barrowfield training ground, stripped and ready for training!.

733. THE FORM OF other players rise and fall like a temperature graph,
but Bobby Lennox is consistency itself. He is a 100% trier all the
time, in every match. **Jock Stein** talking in 1974 about Lennox.

734. " THE DAY we beat Rangers 7-1 **Willie Fernie** was in mesmeris-
ing form. The ball seemed glued to his feet and the Rangers
players could not get near him." Sean Fallon talking about his
colleague Willie Fernie. He was a magic player who played 317
games for Celtic between 1948 and 1961. (he played a few seasons at Middlesborough in the late 1950's, but then came back to
Celtic)

735. ON 19 APRIL 1972, **Dixie Deans** missed a penalty against Inter
Milan in the semi final of the European Cup. Celtic were knocked
out 5-4 in the penalty shoot out. (Craig, Johnstone, McCluskey
and Murdoch scored from the spot). A few days later Celtic played
Motherwell at Celtic Park in the league. Celtic were awarded two
penalties, and the crowd shouted for Dixie to take them. He declined. Bobby Murdoch took both and scored. Celtic won 5-2 and
Dixie also scored two goals.

736. IN 1972 SCOTLAND were on a close season trip to Brazil. The
manager was Tommy Docherty. He picked Celtic midfield player
Steve Murray to go on the tour. But Steve wrote to the SFA
advising that he did not want to go as he had just started an Open
University on Maths and Science, and had a lot of study work
to do. He was known as " Back Seat" by his Celtic team mates,
as he was always studying books up the back of the bus on away
trips. Steve was signed by Jock Stein as a replacement for Bobby
Murdoch. He only played 100 games for Celtic and had to retire
from football due to a foot injury.

737. One of the worst things in football is telling a young lad that you do not think he will make it. That is part of the job I really hate. I remember when I was at St.Mirren I had to let go a lot of young players. One of the kids was close to tears when I told him I was allowing him to move on. I was near to tears myself when he asked me for my autograph and told me I had been his favourite footballer during my playing days. Celtic manager **Davie Hay**

738. I am telling you bhoys that **Jimmy McGrory** scored 54 hat tricks in his career. One of the Celtic fans favourite songs in the 1930's was, " Tell me the old, old story. A hat trick for McGrory! " – **pub football expert.**

739. In 1898 Celtic manager Willie Maley spent £300 on signing forward **John Bell** from Everton. This was a huge amount of money for a football player, and the Glasgow newspaper, the Evening Times, printed a special edition because it was such a big story. He played in the 2-0 Scottish Cup final victory over Rangers in 1899.

740. "Dad, I need to tell you something. My new boy friend is not a Celtic supporter: he took me to Ibrox last week, but, honest, I did not cheer when they scored." a 16 year old ghirl to her Dad.

741. "At least you are a moving target. I am stuck here in the dug out." **Jock Stein** tried to calm Jimmy Johnstone before the semi final of the European Cup against Atletico Madrid in Spain. It was rumoured that a sniper was going to shoot at Jinky.

742. **Stevie Chalmers** scored the most important goal in the history of Celtic in Lisbon in 1967. Stevie made his debut for Celtic in 1959 when he was 22 years old (not a youngster), and went on to score 228 goals during his career with Celtic.

743. " John, you've given me my first night's sleep in months". Celtic chairman Bob Kelly to **John McPhail** after the Scottish Cup

Final game in 1951. John had just scored the winning goal to beat Motherwell 1-0

744. " ANYONE WHO treated **Patsy Gallacher** badly got their own medicine back. Nor did it matter what size the opponent was. The bigger they were the harder they fell to Gallacher " Celtic chairman Bob Kelly

745. "THERE'S PLENTY MORE where that came from". Celtic's **Bertie Auld** to the Leeds United players who surrounded him at Hampden Park in the semi final of the European Cup in 1970. Bertie had just flattened a Leeds player. "Leeds were bullies and wanted to mix it at times. But we were all right with that. We could match them, at least, at the football and we had no fears when it came to the naughty bits."

746. **TOM MCADAM** SIGNED for Celtic in 1977 as a centre forward, but could also play centre half. He had a great scoring record against Rangers. He scored 8 goals. He often played against his brother Colin who played for Rangers. " The Old Firm games were probably more difficult for our parents rather than us. For them the best result would be a 3-3 draw with us both scoring a hat trick."

747. **RUDI VATA** WAS born in Albania. In 1991 he fled to the west after Albania played France in 1991, and he claimed political asylum. He joined Celtic in 1992. He became the first Albanian to win an honour in a major European country when he won the 1995 Scottish Cup with Celtic. The team that day was Bonner; Vata, Boyd, McNally, McKinlay; McLaughlin, Grant, McStay, Collins; Donnelly (O'Donnell 70min), van Hooijdonk (Falconer 39min). It is said that Rudi learned to speak English by watching TV soaps.

748. WHEN WE PLAYED Rangers we were on £1,000 to win, and that was a huge driving force to get players to play. If you were earning £55 basic a week, and you had the chance to earn, £1,000, you

would kill wouldn't you? **Lou Macari** talking about the Celtic bonus structure in the 1970's. The players were on a small basic wage, and had to win to get a regular bonus.

749. The **Lisbon Lions** had a three players who were born in the 1930s: Ronnie Simpson 11/10/1930: Jim Craig 30/04/1943: Tommy Gemmell16/10/1943: Bobby Murdoch 17/08/1944: Billy McNeill 02/03/1940: John Clark 13/03/1941: Jimmy Johnstone 30/09/1944: Willie Wallace 23/06/1940: Stevie Chalmers 26/12/1936: Bertie Auld 23/03/1938: Bobby Lennox 30/08/1943. Substitute John Fallon 16/08/1940. Manager Jock Stein 06/10/1922

750. I remember the less successful years at Celtic Park. The club knew defeat and disappointment. They never knew prejudice, panic, or despair. And win, lose, or draw, they never resorted to power play. Those of us who had to wait for those nine great years thought it was well worth it. I hope there are many great tomorrows for this club. **Frank McElphone**, Minister of Sport for Scotland, speaking in 1976 at a Celtic night in Glasgow City Hall to honour the winning nine-in-a-row league championships.

751. "You are not getting another McDonalds (hamburger) until Marc Fortune scores 30 goals this season. " Celtic fan to his son (aged about 6) when leaving Celtic Park after a game and the wee fella was pleading for a burger.

752. The DVD /movie starring John Hurt called " Shooting Dogs", is the best and most accurate movie made about the genocide in Rwanda. At the very, very end of the movie credits, they show you photos of Tutsi's who were in the movie and who had survived the slaughter, and the very last credit is a gentleman called Hassan wearing his **CELTIC** jersey. I was really chuffed about it. I visit Rwanda frequently and I dish out on behalf of the Joburg Celtic Supporters Club, Celtic gear which we get donated for our proj-

ect ' **Bhoys for Africa**", from Celtic supporters throughout the world. And some people say Celtic is only a football team. **Bill**

753. **JOCK STEIN** PLAYED 148 games for Celtic. When his career was finished due to an ankle injury, he was put in charge of the Celtic reserves. As part of Celtic's youth policy in 1959 they had a team in the league and also had a separate Cup team. They lost 4-0 in the semi final of the Scottish Cup to St.Mirren.

754. IN 1966 CELTIC hosted its own equivalent of the Miss World beauty contest in the Locarno ballroom: The first winner of Miss Celtic was the beautiful **Kathleen English.**

755. AFTER THE 1977 Scottish Cup final at Hampden when Celtic beat Rangers 1-0, **Kenny Dalglish** lost his winners medal during the lap of honour. He stopped to show a few kids sitting in wheelchairs the winners medal and dropped it. He was on his hands and knees with Peter Latchford looking for it, but could not find it. The police told him to go back to the dressing room and they would look for it. It was eventually found in the umbrella of someone at the wheelchair area.

756. "CONGRATULATIONS TO CELTIC for their consistency and contribution to the entertainment value of the League Cup over the years." Scottish League President **Tom Lauchlan** before Celtic played Rangers in the League Cup Final in 1978. This was Celtic's fourteenth consecutive appearance in the final – a world record for a national competition in football.

757. CELTIC PLAYED THE Republic of China international team at Celtic Park in 1979. Celtic won 6-1.

758. I REMEMBER GOING to collect Jimmy Johnstone the night he played his first game as a junior with Blantyre. But he was not at home and had gone to the playground of his local school. There he was kicking the ball against the wall and killing it with one move when

the ball came back to him. If he failed to trap the ball first time, he punished himself by running a lap around the playground. Jimmy had natural talent but he also worked very hard as a youngster to improve himself. **Frank Cairney**, who helped the Boys Guild team in Viewpark where Jimmy was born.

759. I WAS NEARLY spewing by the time I got into the dressing room. I thought we had lost the league championship because of me. If Celtic had lost I thought that was the end of my Celtic career. Then I heard a cheer and the grounds man came into the dressing room and told me we had scored. I suffered in there, and no disciplinary action could have been worse that what I went through. **Johnny Doyle** speaking after Celtic's famous 4-2 win at Celtic Park against Rangers to win the league with 10 men. He was sent off early in the second half.

760. "PAUL MCSTAY IS exceptional. For all their huge investment in players, Rangers simply do not possess a talent to compare with his. McStay is in a class of his own." A journalist writing in Celtic's Centenary Year 1988

761. LUIGI MACARI ONLY played 102 games for Celtic (58 in the league). But he won league championship winners medals in 1970 and 1972: and Scottish Cup winner medals in 1971 and 1972. But he also collected three consecutive League Cup loser medals –1971-73. He was transferred to Manchester United in 1973. Luigi was married in St. Patricks Cathedral in New York in 1970.

762. LISBON LION **STEVE Chalmers** was born on 26 December 1936. He joined Celtic from Ashfield Juniors in 1959. He was 23 years old, which is quite late for a footballer to step up to the senior ranks.

763. IN APRIL 1969 Celtic won the League, the Scottish Cup, and the League Cup, all in the same month. No other team had ever done

this treble in a month. (the League Cup final was usually played in October, but was postponed due to fire damage at Hampden.)

764. CELTIC BEAT ABERDEEN 3-2 in the final of the St.Mungo Cup in July 1951 at Hampden. Celtic were losing 2-0, but came back to win 3-2. **Jimmy Walsh** scored the winner. 80,000 people watched the game and the gate money was £6,000.

765. I HAVE FEW regrets in life, but one is that I never studied at University. So it means a lot to me to be awarded an honorary degree from Glasgow University. It is a magnificent gesture. John Greig and I have been friends for a very long time and we're really looking forward to the ceremony in the summer 2008. **Billy McNeill**

766. LUIGI MACARI PICKED the following players as the best he has played alongside at Celtic and Manchester United : Stepney, McGrain, Gemmell, Murdoch, McNeill, Lennox, Johnstone, Robson, Charlton, Law and Best. Now that is some team!

767. GOALKEEPER **GORDON MARSHALL** signed for Rangers as an apprentice in 1979. He was 18 years old and was loaned to East Stirlingshire to get experience. Gordon played 100 games for Celtic during the 7 years he played for the club.

768. IN 1949 CELTIC played West Ham in London but lost 5-2. But Celtic received praise in the newspapers for their play and it was reported, " Celtic showed how football used to be played in this country, before it was sacrificed on the altar of bash and speed, and it inspired West Ham to play it likewise only West Ham played it faster"

769. TO ME BOBBY Murdoch will go down as one of the finest Celts ever. He was absolutely magnificent and could have played for any team at any level. The phrase "world class" is a bit overused, but

he was that and a little bit more. Sometimes people forget that. – **Bertie Auld**

770. CHARLIE TULLY SHOULD have made a lot of money out of football, but ended up with nothing. One of the reasons was that he was a very generous man. Underneath his colourful character he had a heart of gold. There was never a dull moment when he was here. **Sean Fallon**

771. "I CANNOT BELIEVE the number of wingers who roll around in mock agony when they are tackled. In my day it would never have happened especially under Jock Stein at Celtic Reserves. Stein's gospel to wingers was to never let the full-backs know they had hurt you in challenges. To him it was a sign of weakness and who am I to disagree with the Big Man." **Bobby Carroll** who played for Celtic in the early 1960's. He scored Celtic's first-ever goal in European competition against Valencia in a Fairs Cities Cup-tie at Parkhead, as well as netting in a 1-0 friendly over Everton that was the Hoops' maiden victory in a floodlit game at Celtic Park.

772. THE BEST WAY forward is to attract young players who are not only talented, but want to play for Celtic. But that does not mean that we will not go into the transfer when needed. Celtic chairman **Tom Devlin** gives his views on the future of the club in the 1980's.

773. THE POLAR BEAR trophy is one of the most unusual mementos in the Celtic trophy room. It was presented by Valur of Iceland who Celtic played in the European Cup Winners Cup in 1975. Celtic won 9-0 over the two legs. In the first game in Iceland, Celtic's Icelandic player **Johannes " Shuggie" Edvaldsson** played directly against his brother. Shuggie missed a twice taken penalty kick in this game.

774. ONE OF THE best telephone calls in my life is when I phoned my brother, Gerry, to tell him I had 3 tickets for the UEFA Cup final

in Seville. I think his words were " Oh ya f★★★★★g dancer". Our friend. John Kerr, who we have travelled the world with to some to celebrate St.Patrick's Day in some amazing places, was getting the 3rd ticket. I could imagine John bouncing around like Zebidee in his flat when he heard the news. Every second weekend we watch the Celtic away games in John's flat on the " biggest screen in Glasgow". John is proud of his 52 inch Sony. Even passengers on jets that fly high over Glasgow can see this Wonder of the World. Before the game in Seville, we spent 5 nights in the Portuguese town of Pria de Rocha. My memory of the hotel, which looked like Cell Block H , was every minute of that day and night you could hear the immortal words " Mon the Hoops" being shouted from the window of a party in someone's room. Robert Harvey

775. Jock Stein did not like alcohol. I never touched a drink until I was about 30. I remember once a holiday trip to Jersey and he found out that I had driven some of the older players to a few pubs while I had an orange juice. I still remember the lecture he gave me. I was nearly greetin. **Danny McGrain**

776. Lenny is the official mascot of the Brisbane CSC in Australia. He is named in honour of the Celtic legend **Neil Lennon**. He is an Australian Koala bear, who enjoys watching Celtic, drinking, meeting ghirls and travelling the world in suitcases (free). He adopted the Brisbane CSC when we found him in St Kilda, Melbourne whilst we were attending The Jock Stein CSC get together in June 2006. So far he has been skiing in New Zealand, toured Ireland twice and lived in Dublin and Glasgow for three months each. If any member is heading off anywhere exotic, please take Lenny along and get some photos. www.brisbanecsc.com/mascot.html

777. A manager can work 24 hours a day to try and achieve success, but always remember he is only as good as his players. For me the

most important thing is to know when to share the players' problems and when to leave them alone. **Jock Stein**

778. I KNOW WHAT it is like if a young player gets a free transfer. It is heart breaking, but sadly it has to happen from time to time. I can say to the lad that I know exactly how he is feeling, but I also tell them that they can still make a satisfying career in football even if one particular door has closed on them. Celtic chief scout **John Kelman.** He played at Bolton and Norwich as a youngster, but was never a star. He used to watch seven games a week to identify the best young players to bring to Celtic.

779. " NEXT TO Jock Stein, Fergus McCann was the greatest ever Celt, although not in the way we think of great players." Journalist Hugh Keevins.

780. I FEEL SORRY for young goalkeepers in Glasgow who have to play on ash parks. Landing on a rock hard surface is no joke. You can still be picking red blaize bits out of your arms and legs a week later. Celtic goalkeeper **Pat Bonner**

781. CELTIC CAN'T BE an ordinary team as it came from extraordinary roots and if roots don't flower at the top then they are not worth flowering at all. Actor **John Cairney** who is a big Celtic fan. He was the star of the Celtic Quizball team in the 1960's that won the BBC national quiz twice in a row. The Celtic team was so good (Craig, McNeil, Wallace and Cairney) that they were barred from entering the next series.

782. WE ASKED SIX different experts if it was safe to go there and they came up with slightly different answers. Eventually the consensus was in favour that we should go and play the game. Celtic chairman **Jack McGinn** after Celtic were drawn to play Dynamo Kiev after the nuclear power disaster at Chernobyl.

783. WE ARE ALL really pleased with him. I've always said it requires a strong personality to play at Celtic Park and to see that mental strength in one so young is fantastic. Celtic manager Martin O'Neill talking about 18 year old **Aiden McGeady.** Physical fitness has always been an important part of Celtic's success, but so has mental strength.

784. **HUGH HILLEY** WAS a tough tackling left back who played almost 200 games for Celtic in the 1920's. He had to stop playing due to health problems, but the things he learned from Celtic about diet and fitness stayed with him for the rest of his life. Even as an old man he would have a routine where he would get up at 6 a.m. and have a cold shower, then drink a cup of warm water, then jog around the block, then have some cereal, toast, olive oil and fresh orange. He became a successful business man and launched his famous Hilleys Choc Bar, made of mint, strawberry, vanilla, or coffee, and covered in chocolate.

785. "I DON'T REALLY suffer from nerves. As long as I have a wee piece of chewing gum, then I am fine. " Celtic goalkeeper **Allen McKnight**. He played in goal in the Scottish Cup final against Dundee United in the Celtic Centenary year 1988. Celtic won 2-1.

786. " THAT IS what he is paid for." This was always **Jock Stein's** reply to any journalist who asked a question or made a comment about a great save from a Celtic goalkeeper.

787. IT WAS IN a town square in Seville on the day of UEFA Cup Final. It was lunch time and the square was a sea of green and white, with fans enjoying themselves in the sun. Suddenly a car came along the road at the square: a wee Spanish boy, dressed in a Hoops jersey was hanging out the car window waving and smiling at all the Celtic fans. Everyone started waving at the wee fella, and started singing a Celtic song for him. His Dad got out the car, clapped

his hands to applaud the fans, and then drove off into Seville City Centre. It was magical moment in a magical day and made me proud to support Celtic. **Arlene, Glasgow**

788. **Jimmy Johnstone** was sent off against Rangers in the New Year's Day game in 1965. He got fed up being kicked, and punched a Rangers player named Theo Beck. The referee was the famous " giant" Tom Wharton. " Name ?" he said to Jinky. " Roy Rogers" replied Jinky as he was sent to the dressing room. (Roy Rogers was a famous American cowboy singer at that time).

789. Accuracy of passing the ball was everything. If you passed the ball to one of the senior players it had to be right. When you passed to Peter Wilson and it was not right, he would not chase after it. He would shout at you, and tell you to win the ball back. That was the way you were punished, so that the next time you made sure you gave a good pass. **Malcom McDonald**, who many older Celtic supporters say was one of the true great players for Celtic.

790. You will get your first breath about ten o'clock tonight. Bobby Lennox joked with young **Peter Grant**, after young Peter was told he was making his debut in the Old Firm game at Ibrox later that day.

791. I must be the first player to pee champagne after an Old Firm game. **Joe Miller** after he scored the winning goal against Rangers in the 1989 Scottish Cup final. Joe's name came out the hat along with 3 other players (two Rangers players) to have a mandatory drug test after the game. He was so dehydrated that he could not provide a sample, but he just kept drinking champagne until he could pee. He passed the test no problem.

792. **Bobo Balde** loved to play the guitar as a way of relaxing away from football. He liked to play the blues music, especially John Lee Hooker.

793. I FELT A bit scared when I came home from the meeting with Mr.McGinn and Mr.Cassidy, during which I accepted the manager's job. I was given a video showing the history of Celtic and after watching it I became scared again. But that fear soon disappeared and I am just looking forward to the job. New Celtic manager **Liam Brady** in June 1991

794. MARTIN O'NEILL DID have one thing going for him when he arrived up there in Glasgow – he didn't need to work too hard to get fans to come to the ground. All he had to do was tell them it was Saturday. What a luxury, massive home crowds virtually guaranteed. Brian Clough when his former player **Martin O'Neill** became manager at Celtic.

795. IN THE SEMI final of the Glasgow Cup, which was a prestigious tournament, in 1942, Celtic were awarded 3 penalties against Rangers, but missed 2 of them.

796. **JIMMY McGRORY** LEAVES memories of the finest and of deeds in our colours that will never fade. Celtic manager Willie Maley in 1938 when Jimmy left to be manager of Kilmarnock

797. THE BEST JOB in Glasgow in April 2003 was a Beach Ball salesman. It is about Supply and Demand. When 30,000 people are looking for a green and white beach ball, prices will get higher. **Pub football expert.** Celtic fans took their (beach) balls to Ibrox just after Celtic had qualified for the UEFA final, and showered the park when the teams came out. The game was held up while they were cleared. On the Monday after the game there was lots of calls from Celtic supporters to Ibrox asking, " Can I have my ball back?". The phone was eventually slammed down.

798. " IT WAS the daftest question I have ever asked." **Frank McAvennie** talking about the time he was in a night club in London with the great George Best. He asked George if he ever regretted not playing in the World Cup finals. George was sitting surrounded by

beautiful women. " Not really" replied George, " I have slept with three beautiful Miss.World's, so that will do me!"

799. IF CELTIC DO well on the field, it will not be worth it if the supporters cannot or will not behave decently. **Jock Stein**. He detested bad behaviour.

800. "AND ALL THE stars that never were, are parking cars and pumping gas." **Fergus McCann**'s reply to a journalist who asked if he was worried about losing his star players on pre-contract agreements. It is a line from the song Do You Know the Way to San Jose

801. MY TEAM WOULD lose games where it became a scrap. Martin always wins. Ex Celtic manager Liam Brady compared his team to Martin O'Neills team.

802. JOCK STEIN'S KNOWLEDGE of football was immense, and he paid attention to small things that others ignored. He also knew how to handle players, and was not afraid of the big games, which is a great strength. **Pat Stanton** talking about his manager Jock Stein.

803. IF THE TWO ladies who were not happy with our performance want to contact me I will treat them to lunch at Celtic Park and we can discuss further. Celtic manager **Tommy Burns** after they complained to him in the dugout at Firhill when Celtic drew 0-0 with Partick Thistle

804. "YOU SHOULD HAVE seen it, there was thousands of them running down Kent Street from Lynch's bar. Honestly it looked like Zulu Dawn. Big Pierre van Hooijdonk was astonished at the scene. Now he knows what Celtic Football Club is all about." Celtic manager **Tommy Burns** speaking after Celtic beat Airdrie 1-0 to win the Scottish Cup in 1995. The Celtic bus took the route back to Celtic Park with the cup that Jock Stein took his team back in 1965. Down the Gorbals, past the Brazen Head, and then

right along the Gallowgate, past Bairds Bar and the Calton, down London Rd, and up Kerrydale Street. There were thousands of Celtic supporters celebrating.

805. CELTIC MANAGER JOHN Barnes signed Brazilian defender **Rafael Scheidt** in December 1999 from Gremio for £4.8 million. The green Brazilian played a total of 6 games in his Celtic career – two starts and four substitute appearances, before being released. His father got upset when Celtic made the understandable decision to put only his first name on the back of his jersey.

806. "THE NEW CELTIC Park is a family stadium for every man, woman, and child. It is fabulous and I defy any stadium in the world to match the atmosphere it has now – even Ally McCoist said that to me !". **Elaine C. Smith**, Scottish entertainer, who is a big Celtic fan.

807. I AM A better player and a better person for my time with Borussia Dortmund. I live life differently. I now understand that if you don't go with the methods and regimes of the top players, you get left behind. I also learned one of the main things is that you win as a team and lose as a team. **Paul Lambert** when he joined Celtic.

808. A FEW YEARS ago a Celtic Memorabilia Pack was issued. It contained things like a letter signed by Jimmy McGrory in 1946 to Bury football Club: the programme from the Celtic Supporters Association first annual rally and concert in 1951: the official match programme from the 1938 Exhibition Cup Final against Everton: the itinerary of the Celtic tour to America in 1966: a tribute card from Willie Maley to John Thomson : the Evening Citizen newspaper dated 26 May 1967 with Jock Stein and the European Cup; Picture of Celtic versus Hearts game on 04 January 1910: the first Celtic View in August 1965: official match program of the 1953

Celtic versus Hibs Coronation Cup Final: the contract signed by John Stein when he joined Celtic in 1953.

809. HE WAS THE greatest menace to goalkeepers in the history of football. Celtic historian James Handley talking about **Jimmy McGrory**

810. CELTIC HIRED SCOTTISH artist Alasdair Gray to design the front cover of the Celtic View magazine for the clubs first ever UEFA Champions League game against Rosenborg on 12 September 2001. The cover featured drawings of the faces of Jock Stein, Martin O'Neill, Henrik Larsson and the European Cup trophy. The background was orange. It was a work of art, but not everyone liked it. (The game was postponed due to the 9/11 attack on New York's Twin Towers).

811. **JOE McBRIDE** WAS nicknamed " Marlon Brando" by French journalists when Celtic played Nantes in the European Cup because of his resemblance to the Hollywood actor.

812. I WILL NEVER forget the night after I scored at Ibrox. I got quite drunk in a Chinese restaurant. I then kept falling asleep, and the waiters were shaking me to wake up. All I kept saying/singing was " Who put the ball in the Rangers net, I did, I did", **Tony Cascarino** scored at Ibrox in a 1-1 in November 1991. He scored 4 goals in 30 games during his career at Celtic.

813. **ALAN THOMPSON** WAS a tough tackling, goal scoring midfield player who manager Martin O'Neill signed for Celtic from Aston Villa in 2000. His dad used to bet a few pounds on him scoring when Celtic played Rangers. Alan described the best goal he scored against Rangers for three reasons: One, it was in the last minute. Two, because it was against Rangers. Three it bent round Ricksen on the way into the net. (Alan always had tough games against Fernando Ricksen of Rangers).

814. " THIS IS massive. I woke up on Friday morning with a big smile on my face and it is such a tremendous feeling." **Henrik Larsson** the morning after he scored the only goal against Boavista in Portugal to put Celtic through to the UEFA Cup final in 2003.

815. THE FIRST PRESS box built to accommodate football reporters was created by Celtic in 1894

816. " IT IS our proud boast that we can taste the fruits of victory in the same spirit as the bitterness of defeat ". Celtic manager **Willie Maley**

817. IN THE LATE 1890's Celtic put a protective cover of straw over the pitch to protect the ground from heavy frost and to avoid postponement of games.

818. " MCGRORY HIT the post with a hard shit". There used to be early editions of the news papers, for example the Green Citizen or Pink Evening Times, for sale at 6 o'clock on a Saturday night. These had match reports of games that had just finished an hour earlier. Fans used to wonder how the newspaper companies could produce them so quickly. They were full of misprints and spelling mistakes, but were good summaries of the games.

819. A GHOST-WRITTEN BOOK by Celtic's **Shunsuke Nakamura** containing his reflections on life is widely read in Japanese schools and has also become recommended reading by the Japanese government. His biography " The Zen Of Naka," was also translated and published in Japan. The Japanese football supporters have a fascination with the role of football in the UK, especially the Celtic-Rangers rivalry. Naka's personal qualities of humility and dedication are much appreciated in Japan, as well as his skills as a footballer.

820. "WHEN I WATCHED Ronnie Simpson being taken off even before the game started, I stood there and knew something was wrong

with me, and then it struck me what it was – I was terrified."
Jimmy Johnstone talking about the World Club championship game in Buenos Aires against Racing Club of Argentina.
Goalkeeper Simpson had been hit in the head by a missile thrown
from the crowd.

821. Roy Kay HAS the shortest name of any player to have played in
the Celtic first team. He was a full back signed from Hearts in
1977. Roy played 10 games for Celtic.

822. This club has been my life and I feel without it my existence
would be empty indeed. **Willie Maley**

823. On 10 September 1985 at Ninian Park Cardiff, Jock Stein's life
ended as it he had lived it – through football. He died of a heart
attack at the dugout during a Scotland versus Wales World Cup
match. Twenty years after this tragic episode a group of football
fans arranged for a plaque to be erected in the away dugout at
Ninian Park. It reads: "**In respectful memory of Jock Stein
who sadly left football forever while managing Scotland at
Ninian Park on 10 September 1985. From football fans all
over the world**." Jock was cremated at the Linn Crematorium
in Glasgow.

824. Glasgow pubs were allocated a licence to serve alcohol until
11.15pm on the night of the match. (Celtic v Feyenoord European
Cup Final in 1970. There were however two conditions. The
first was that publicans must apply to the Chief Constable and the
Town Clerk for permission. The second condition was that the
pub must have a television set. **www.stateofthegame.co.uk**

825. In 1973 Celtic missed 5 penalties in a row. Murdoch, Dalglish,
and Hood all missd in the same game against East Fife. Murdoch
missed against Airdrie, Dalglish missed against Kilmarnock.

826. " WONDERFUL INSIGHT into the history of this proud club and it's
      loyal supporters. Funny, moving and hugely entertaining, whatev-
      er your historical roots are." Celtic fan John Crook from Dunblane
      gives his opinion on the Celtic Story play at the Pavilion Theatre
      in Glasgow which ran from 29 July to 05 September 1998

827. "YOU BETTER BE quick. He will probable get the sack next week."
      A Celtic fan on a tour of the stadium at Celtic Park had stopped
      manager **Gordon Strachan** and asked him to have his photo-
      graph taken with him. He made this comment as the photo was
      being taken. Strachan was new into the managers job and Celtic
      had just lost five goals to Artmedia Bratislava and four goals to
      Motherwell. The fans comment was meant to be a joke, but it hit a
      nerve with Strachan, who then threw the fan out of Celtic Park.

828. CELTIC SIGNED LEFT winger **Andy Lynch** from Hearts in 1973. He
      once scored four goals for Celtic in a reserve game against Rangers
      which Celtic won 4-3. Andy eventually was converted into a left
      back and played 185 games for Celtic. He scored the winning goal
      in the 1977 Scottish Cup Final against Rangers from the penalty
      spot. Celtic won 1-0.

829. **DAVIE ADAMS** WAS the Celtic goalkeeper when Celtic won the
      league six times in a row between 1905-1910. One day Celtic
      lost a goal and a supporter shouted " You're no a good goalie", "
      Maybe no" replied Davie, " but the Celtic Board don't know it
      yet"

830. BROTHER WALFRID WAS born Andrew Kerins in Ballymote in Sligo
      in West of Ireland on May 18 1840. At 24 years old he joined the
      Marist Priests Teaching Order. It is thought that he chose his name
      after Galfrido Della Gherardesca a wealthy man from Pisa in Italy
      who was called to a religious life, and who was later canonised
      St.Walfrid.

831. " You CANNOT win with eighty per cent of the team off form. We went out expecting things to happen. That was wrong. The Dutch went out and made things happen. We did not stretch them as we should have. It was something special for Feyenoord. For us, it seemed to be just an ordinary game. " **Jock Stein** after Celtic lost 2-1 to Feyenoord in the European Cup final in Milan in 1970.

832. " WHAT MAKES a great player? It is a question that I am often asked and my answer is always the same. He is one who brings out the best in others, and when I am saying that I am talking about Billy McNeill. It is this quality of bringing the units of the team to-gether, and inspiring them to play for each other and for the club, which has raised our captain above all others in the past decade." **Jock Stein** writing in the match program for the Billy McNeill testimonial game against Liverpool in 1974.

833. WHEN CELTIC WON the European Cup in 1967, as the holders they automatically qualified for the competition the next season, and they did not have to pay the entry fee of 200 Swiss francs (which was sixteen pounds and ten shillings).

834. IN THE EARLY 1950's Celtic were playing Hibs at Easter Road in a league game. Hibs were a great team with the Famous Five for-ward line. Hibs were awarded 4 penalties in the game and Eddie Turnbull scored 4 goals. **Johnny Bonnar** was the Celtic goal-keeper. " The last penalty nearly tore my hands off as it went into the net!"

835. "PEOPLE SAY HE lacks a yard in pace, but I say to them that he is ten yards quicker upstairs than other players." Tommy Docherty talking about **Kenny Dalglish**

836. ON CHRISTMAS DAY 1967 France Football Magazine voted Celtic's left back **Tommy Gemmell** the sixth best player in Europe. In 1970 a poll of sports journalists in Hungary and Brazil (two of

the nations renowned for their attacking style of football) voted
Tommy as the best right back in the world. Tommy played for
Celtic between 1961 and 1971 and considered it a poor season if he
did not score at least 10 goals.

837.   " CELTIC WILL always be one of the great loves of my life." **Pat
Crerand**.

838.   ONE DAY MR.STEIN played me at full back and I did well. He obviously felt this was my natural position. I was surprised how easily
I fitted into the role. If he had not noticed this potential in me, I
might have drifted along as an average mid field player. **Danny
McGrain.**

839.   "IT'S A REAL honour for us to welcome the Lisbon Lions. They're
an iconic team with a great story to tell." Kevin Moore, Preston's
Museum Director when the Lions visited Preston North End.

840.   FILES ABOUT   **JOCK Stein** were been released by The Scottish
Government under Freedom of Information (National Archives
of Scotland ref. ED33/23). The released file concerns the period
following the 1967 European Cup win, when consideration was
given by Scottish Government officials to proposing Stein for an
Honour after the club's victory. The Scottish Office recommended that Stein should be granted a CBE, and later proposals were
put forward for a knighthood for contributions to Scottish football
(NAS ref. ED33/23 p29). The argument ran that other football
managers such as Sir Alf Ramsay, the England manager, and later
Sir Matt Busby of Manchester United, had received similar honours following their respective footballing successes. The recommendation included a supporting statement that: **"Celtic is the
first British club even to reach the final of the European
Cup and it is widely acknowledged that Mr Stein's tactical
ability has been decisive in this achievement."** A further re-
vised handwritten amendment added that; **"The attacking play**

of the club under his guidance has been as attractive as it has been successful and has had a salutory influence on the defensive style which had characterised the European competitions in recent years." (NAS ref. ED33/23 p10). The recommendation was turned down at the time, though Jock was eventually awarded a CBE in 1970. http://www.nas.gov.uk/about/070629new.asp

841. "WITH HEART in hand and Pat Crerand, we'll cut off King William's balls". Celtic supporters used to sing about **Paddy Crerand** in the early 1960s.

842. IT IS THE same the world over – when fathers and sons run out of things to talk about, they can always talk about football. A father and son don't often say that they love each other but they can swear undying allegiance to their favourite team, especially if that team is the Glasgow Celtic. That's how you learn the history – by talking to your Dad. **Pub football expert**

843. "GOALKEEPERS COME AND goalkeepers go, but there is still only one Tiger." Charlie Tully talking about team mate **John Bonnar**, who played nearly 200 games for Celtic between 1948 and 1958. His greatest game was Celtic's victory in the Coronation Cup final against Hibs.

844. ON 16 JANUARY 1971 Celtic beat Dundee 8-1 at Dens Park. Celtic were winning 2-0 at half time. In the second half Jinky was on fire on the wing and Celtic scored six more goals. Six goals came from getting to the bye line and crossing the ball into the danger area. It was inspired wing play.

845. **SEAN FALLON** WHO came from Sligo, was given the Freedom of Sligo in 2002. He was a great Celt.

846. "THERE IS no disgrace at all for us. This was a great victory by a team that has everything". Hibs manager Bob Shankly talking af-

ter Celtic beat his team 5-3 at Easter Road in October 1966. This
was one of the great games of the 60's. **Joe McBride** scored four
goals in the game, and **Steve Chalmers** scored one goal.

847. **WILLIE HUGHES** PLAYED 100 games for Celtic in the early 1930's.
      He was an outside left. He scored 8 goals in the benefit game for
      the great Patsy Gallacher in January 1932.

848. JIMMY McGRORY WAS our manager and he was a gentleman. He
      had total respect of all the players at Celtic Park. I still smile when
      I think of some of the advice he used to give us players as we left
      the dressing room before a match. After comments to 10 players
      he ran out of positive things to say, and Mike Haughney who was
      always last to leave, would be told " well cheerio then Mike."
      Bobby Evans.

849. "I CANNOT RECALL seeing a player with such speed and stamina. I
      rate him as one of the best I have ever seen.". The great Hungarian
      striker Ference Bene talking about **Tommy Callaghan** after
      Celtic played Ujpest Dozsa. Tommy played up and down the left
      side of the pitch on his own; he had incredible running power and
      talent, but was not always appreciated by the supporters.

850. **PATSY GALLACHER** PLAYED 464 games for Celtic and scored 196
      goals. He was one of the great players. He had a pub in Clydebank
      and was generous to people who were short of money. When he
      died, it was found that he had a safe drawer in his pub stacked with
      IOUs for hundreds of pounds that accumulated over the years and
      had never bothered to collect.

851. **CHARLIE NICHOLAS** WAS a phenomenon when he first came into
      the Celtic team. He was probably the best young player in Europe.
      He could have gone on to become one of the world's best strik-
      ers, but he should never have left Celtic when he did. **Tommy
      Burns**

852. THE FIRST COMPETITIVE Old Firm game was on 27 October 1888 when Celtic beat Rangers 6-1 at Ibrox in the third round of the Glasgow Cup. It is still a record away win. The goal scorers were Mick Dunbar (2), Tom Maley, Johnny Coleman, James Kelly and Willie Groves

853. " I GOT my retaliation in first." **Patsy Gallacher**. Defenders used to think that they could kick The Mighty Atom out of a game, but they were in for a surprise.

854. "IF I WIN the half time raffle with that number, there is no way I am going out onto the park to collect my money". A Celtic fan on his way into a league game with St.Johnsone in August 2009 at Celtic Park. He had just bought a Celtic raffle ticket with a first prize of £9,000. If his number was selected it was displayed on the Big Screen and he would have to go onto the park and collect his cheque. The number of his raffle ticket was 1690. **Dougie Lynch**

855. IN 1993 a street has been was named after Celtic goalkeeper John Thomson. It is called Thomson Court. In the old part of Bowhill Cemetery in Fife, not far from the gate, you can see a memorial erected in his memory. The inscription reads: IN MEMORIAM: **JOHN THOMSON**: SCOTLAND'S INTERNATIONAL GOALKEEPER, who died 5th September 1931 aged 22 years. The result of injuries received at Ibrox Park. Beloved son of John and Jean Thomson. "Honest and upright he played the game. Beloved and respected he made his name".

856. WE WERE PLAYING a tour game in Vienna. Jimmy disappeared off the park and he came back on about ten minutes later. I shouted to him, " What is wrong wee man, where have you been?" He replied straight faced, " I was bursting for the toilet and I just had to go." **Tommy Gemmell** talking about **Jimmy Johnstone**.

857. **DAN McARTHUR** MAY the best goalkeeper ever to play for Celtic. He had a 30% shutout record, and played 120 games. Dan was only 5 ft 5 in tall, but was a fearless keeper.

858. **JOCK STEIN** WAS famous for clearing his lines with his knee: he could knee a ball as far as some players could kick it.

859. **JOE DODDS** WAS one of the fastest left backs in Celtic's history. He could give most wingers a few yards of a start and beat them in a sprint. Joe played 378 games between 1908 and 1922 and won seven league championship winners medals. He formed the famous full back partnership with Alex McNair. He was an early Tommy Gemmell with a strong shot and scored a remarkable 30 goals in an era when the job of a full back was to defend.

860. HE ALWAYS TOLD us to help out a team mate who was not having the best of games. He told us that it might be our turn in the next game to need assistance. **Billy McNeill** talking about manager Jock Stein

861. " OF ALL the great Celts that have passed away, he has an honoured place" Willie Maley talking about goalkeeper **John Thomson**

862. **JACK KENNEDY** SIGNED for Celtic for £5,000 the day after Jock Stein became Celtic manager in 1965. He was a goalkeeper who the previous year had played for the Great Britain team at the Olympic games in Tokyo. Jack played only one game for the Celtic firs team. He moved to Lincoln City in 1967 where he played over 250 games.

863. THE NIGHT CELTIC were beat by Inverness Caledonian Thistle, which caused manager John Barnes to lose his job, was the first time that Kenny Dalglish had not been in the dressing room at half time. He was in La Manga, Spain. Trouble blew up in the dressing room and Mark Viduka did not re emerge onto the field after half time. It is said he refused to put his jersey on and play the

second half. Kenny would have sorted that out if he had been in that dressing room that night.

864. " THE ONLY way I will go to England is for a holiday." Celtic's Italian star **Paulo Di Canio** a few months before he engineered a move for himself to Sheffield Wednesday in 1997 and let down a lot of Celtic fans.

865. " HE COULDN'T run and he couldn't jump, but by God he could play football. He must be the best passer of a football ever to play in the British Isles. " Celtic goalkeeper Evan Williams talking about **Bobby Murdoch**

866. " HE LIKES to play, train, and then just go home. When he is playing he is prepared to run 80 yards to give a team mate two yards of space." Celtic manager Gordon Strachan talking about **Paul Telfer** who joined Celtic when he was 34 years old. He was a very unselfish player, who always played for the team. Paul was the fittest player at Celtic Park. One of his hobbies was cross country running. He was unusual for a footballer in that he also preferred to watch golf or National Geographic programs on TV rather than a live football match.

867. **JIMMY JOHNSTONE** HAD such a big heart for a small guy. You see wee guys in the modern game and a lot of them feign injury, but no matter how hard someone hit Jimmy he always got up and got on with it. If he was as big as his heart then he would have been ten feet tall. **Tom Boyd**.

868. CELTIC MANAGER **MARTIN O'Neill** was a fan of Gaelic football. He said that he was better at that than he was at football when he was younger.

869. CELTIC PLAYED RANGERS in the famous " Beach Ball" game before going to Seville for the UEFA Cup final. In his book " Man and Bhoy" **Neil Lennon** describes what happened before the game. "

As the team bus approached Ibrox we came to a round about near
Ibrox stadium, and in the middle was a Celtic fan sitting on a deck
chair pretending to sun himself. Next to him was a Celtic fan
using a foot pump to blow up an inflatable crocodile. Inside the
stadium there was loads of beach balls and fans dressed in ponchos
and sombreros. "

870. CELTIC HAVE HAD 17 managers: Willie Maley 1897 to 1940: Jimmy
McStay 1940 to 1945: Jimmy McGrory 1945 to 1965: Jock Stein
1965-1978 (Sean Fallon was caretaker during season 1975-76):
Billy McNeill 1978-1983; David Hay 1983-1987: Billy McNeill
1987-1991; Liam Brady 1991-193; Lou Macari 1993-1994;
Tommy Burns 1994-1997; Wim Jansen 1997-1998; Josef Venglos
1998-1999; John Barnes 1999-2000; Martin O'Neill 2000-2005:
Gordon Strachan 2005-2009: Tony Mowbray 2009 – present. –
This includes Sean Fallon when he was care taker manager when
Jock Stein was in hospital after his near fatal car crash.   (Frank
Connor also had a few games as the caretaker manager in the
1980's)

871. WE PRACTICED SHOOTING all the time in training, but not always
from straight in front of goal. The full backs and mid field players
would often blast balls in diagonally and the strikers had to hit
them first time at different heights. Jock Stein was always stressing
that we had to get shots on target. **Bobby Lennox**

872. " PADDY IS a magnificent talent. What we have to do is work on
his fitness. He is the type of player you have to free in a game. He
is a Lubo Moravcik type." Celtic coach Willie McStay talking
about **Paddy McCourt** who Celtic signed from Derry City in
2008.

873. WHEN **ROBERT DUVALL**, the megastar Hollywood actor, first met
Jimmy Johnstone he loved his company. Duvall was an acclaimed
actor and one of his best parts was as the lawyer to Don Corleone

in The Godfather movie. One night when he was in the East End of Glasgow, Duvall was looking for Jinky and went into a few bars that he knew that Jinky occasionally visited. As he was leaving one of them, someone at the bar said, " Wee Jimmy must be in right trouble now, even the Godfather is looking for him !"

874. CELTIC GOALKEEPER **JONATHAN Gould** did not like to do his pre match warm up routine in front of the actual goal posts. He was superstitious and did not like losing a goal. He took any shots fired into him by the goalkeeping coach by positioning himself to the side of the goals on the bye line.

875. WHEN **SHUNSUKE NAKAMURA** signed for Celtic the fans started a new song: " There's is only one Nakamura, one Nakamra. He eats chow mein and he votes Sinn Fein. Walking in a Naka wonderland."

876. " THE PROBLEM is that it is difficult to make comparisons in different eras, so I don't know who to pick. I'm just delighted that I was part of a very good team and in that respect I would be a bit cheeky and vote for the rest of my Lisbon Lion team mates." This was the answer from **Jimmy Johnstone** when he was asked who he was voting for in the survey in 2001 to pick the Greatest Celtic player of all time.

877. **JIMMY WALSH** SCORED the first televised goal in Scottish football history, when he scored in the 1955 Scottish Cup final at Hampden against Clyde. The game ended in a 1-1 draw. 100,00 spectators were at that game. Jimmy also scored in all 5 games played within a two week period in 1951 when Celtic won the St.Mungo Cup. He also scored in the Coronation Cup final in 1953 against Hibs. (Celtic beat Arsenal and Manchester United in the previous two games). Jimmy played 144 games for Celtic and scored 59 goals. He is part of the Celtic history because of the times he scored his goals.

878. CHARLIE NICHOLAS WAS one of the most naturally gifted players that I have ever played with. He had total confidence in his own ability. Old Firm matches are difficult to play in because everyone is so tense. Not so Charlie. He used to go for nutmegs and would try spectacular things that everyone else was frightened to attempt. **Davie Provan**

879. IN1975 LEEDS UNITED made a £240,000 bid for Kenny Dalglish, which would have been a record transfer at that time. At the same time Jock Stein had done a deal with Dundee United manager Jim McLean for the two best young players in Scotland, David Narey and Andy Gray, for £100,000, But the Celtic board wanted Jock to pay only £60,000 for the two players, which United turned down. These 2 young hungry players would have been great players for Celtic. Kenny was sold to Liverpool two years later.

880. " PETER GRANT of Celtic" is now a thing of the past. I wanted that phrase on my tombstone, but I am a Norwich City player now, although no one can ever take away from me the fact that I am first and foremost a Celtic supporter. Right up to the end I still got a thrill driving along London Road and turning into Kerrydale Street". **Peter Grant**

881. LISBON LION **JIM Craig** signed for Celtic straight from Glasgow University, where he was studying to be a dentist. One day he was doing some sprint training with Jimmy Johnstone who asked him, " How are you getting on at Uni?". "Fine " was Jim's reply. Jinky then said, " It must be murder speaking Latin all the time in your lectures". It was unusual at that time for a footballer to also be at University.

882. "NEXT TO PELE, he was the finest player I ever saw." Celtic fan Thomas McSorley talking about **Charlie Tully**

883. **BILLY CONNOLLY** OPENED the East End stand at Celtic Park with Pete St John in August 1996. He was then invited to join The

Huddle with the players in the centre circle. He does not tell anyone what was said in there.

884. WHEN WERE ON the ground staff at Celtic each day we had different duties such as cleaning the boots to blowing up the balls. But Peter Grant excelled in cleaning the lavvies. He seemed to love it and I will always remember him with his head down the pan scrubbing away. **Paul McStay**.

885. " A WEEK in Spain? It is a f*****g week in Barlinnie that you all need." This was shouted from the crowd when Celtic played Aberdeen at Pittodrie in May 2009. Celtic had just returned from a week's warm weather training in the south of Spain, but were not playing very well in the first half against the Dons. Celtic eventually won the game 3-1. **Ann Lennon**

886. ALL THE PLAYERS have been great in helping me settle in at Celtic. At the end of the day a dressing room is a dressing room. There are obviously more experienced top class players here than at Motherwell, but you get the same kind of jokes and chat. Although it was a bit weird sitting in there with the likes of Henrik Larsson before the game on Saturday, having supported Celtic all my life. But I'll get used to it. " **Stephen Pearson** when he signed from Motherwell. He was a very direct midfield player, who liked to run at defenders at high speed with the ball, set up chances, and get shots at goal.

887. WE WOULD HAVE played on a bit of spare ground for Celtic for nothing, such was the desire to play for the club. **Bertie Auld**

888. "HENRIK LARSSON IS the best all round player that I have ever played with. There is no edge or arrogance to him. On the pitch he is the most unselfish player I have ever worked with." **Chris Sutton** talking about his striking partner at Celtic. Before joining Celtic, Chris had played for a number of English clubs (Norwich, Blackburn, Chelsea) and had been transferred for over 20 million

pounds in his career. He gained a place in British football's history books as the first £5 million transfer between two British clubs. This occurred in July 1994 when he joined Blackburn Rovers from Norwich. In 1999 Chelsea signed him for £10 million. In July 2000 Celtic signed him for £6 million.

889. I USED TO sleep with the ball when I was growing up. The first thing I would do every morning was check if it was still there. Football was your outlet. There was nothing else. **Jimmy Johnstone**

890. THE " GREEN Pages " is a fanzine for Celtic supporters in Germany – see www.celticfc.de/

891. FOLLOWING HIS INVOLVEMENT in a car crash near Lockerbie in the 70s, big Jock Stein was in hospital and all tubed up, so unable to speak. Neilly Mochan visits him on the Saturday after a game at Celtic Park and Jock writes on a note "What was the score, Neilly?". Neilly shouts his answer, then takes the pen and writes "We won 3-1, boss" and hands the note to Jock to read. Jock takes the pen again and writes something else on the note and hands it back to Neilly to read. It says "I'm no deaf, ya daft bugger "

892. **STILIYAN PETROV** WAS lonely in Glasgow when he first joined Celtic from Bulgarian club CSKA Sofia. He did not speak any English, and his Celtic career started badly, mainly because manager John Barnes played him at right back. He used to work in a friend's burger van in the North of Glasgow, and piled on the weight through comfort eating of chicken and hamburgers. He served customers from behind the counter, and he could see the confused look on some faces when he served them. " That cannot be a Celtic player serving in a burger van"

893. " I AM going to freshen things up". The defenders used to smile when they heard **Jock Stein** saying this. This meant he was going to change the forward line, and keep the defenders unchanged.

Jock liked to keep his forwards mentally and physically sharp and freshened up the team often.

894. PICTURE THE SCENE. It is a Govan court and the accused is being questioned by a lawyer, who has a posh accent: **Lawyer** – " You said that you went to your friend's house that night. Why did you go there? ": **Accused**: " Tae get a tap": **Lawyer**: " Is your friend a plumber?".: **Accused,** " Naw. He's just ma pal" : **Lawyer,** " Are you a plumber?": **Accused,** " No me matey": The lawyer then changes his line of questions: **Lawyer,** " So, did you go to borrow money?"; **Accused**: " I wis just back fae the dole, I didnae need any money": The lawyer was now becoming frustrated. " You have told the court that you went to your friends house for a tap. What kind of tap was it?" **Accused:** " It wis a Rangers tap ".

895. I COULD HAVE continued to play with the amateurs of Queens Park, but I don't like that club. That's my right. I have always had a soft spot for Celtic and followed all their matches when I was a kid. I like the Celtic atmosphere. Nothing gives me greater pleasure than to thrash Rangers. So I play for Celtic. **Willie Lyon** . He signed for Celtic in 1935 and was as hard as nails centre half. Willie was captain of the team that won the Empire Exhibition Trophy. In Word War Two he received a bad leg wound at Normandy and this ended his football career.

896. BEFORE A GAME I always tell myself that it will hurt and that it should hurt. I know that I am strong, that I am stronger than them. Even if it hurts, it is going to hurt the opposition even more. **Henrik Larsson** describes how he prepares for a match.

897. I HAVE A funny feeling that I will miss this place more than it will miss me. **Martin O'Neill** when he left Celtic in 2005.

898. "I AM OFTEN asked how the Rangers 'nine in a row' team compares with Celtic's Lisbon Lions of 1967. I have to be honest and

say I think it would be a draw, but then some of us are getting on for 60 years old now " **Bertie Auld**

899. WE HAD A great relationship over the years and I still hear it when I play here in Sweden [Helsingborg]. I still hear the songs over here and sometimes the Celtic jersey is going to be somewhere up in the stand and I always smile when I see it because it's just fantastic. **Henrik Larsson**

900. " EVERY CLUB in Britain should employ a man of his calibre." **Lou Macari** talking about the importance of Sean Fallon in everything Celtic achieved in the 1960's and 1970's. Sean was the assistant manager to Jock Stein.

901. " I SOMETIMES wish I had not bothered.!" **Bobby Murdoch** used to joke about Graeme Souness who became manager at Rangers. When Souness was a young player at Middlesborough he learned a lot about how to be a professional footballer from Bobby. Souness said that Bobby was " a major influence on my career, who regularly passed on advice and told me when he thought I was acting wrongly."

902. JIMMY MCGRORY BROUGHT me to Celtic. He laid the foundation of everything Celtic did later. He knows the club inside out. **Ronnie Simpson**

903. CELTIC BEAT RANGERS 3-1 at Celtic Park on the New Years Day game on 01 January 1900, which was the first Old Firm game of the new century. The goal scorers were Jack Bell and Johnny Divers (2).

904. TONY CASCARINO WAS signed for £1.1 million pounds in 1991 from Aston Villa. He was not a success at Celtic and says it was his biggest regret in football that he did not stay longer at Celtic. His original career choice was to be a hairdresser and not a footballer.

905. "WE LOOKED LIKE racoons." **Charlie Tully**. In 1951 Celtic were on tour in America and played several games under flood lights. The players were not used to this and put on cork eye shadow to avoid reflection.

906. THE ONLY WORRY I had out there in the Lisbon final was the danger of sunstroke. Celtic goalkeeper **Ronnie Simpson**

907. A BRIEF YET concise summary of the Celtic story, a story of a heritage rich beyond the value of words. Celtic has and always will be a traditional and ethical institution, who's mission statement aspires to social integration and the allocation of funds to charitable causes, a club open to all regardless of race or religion. One of only a handful of prestigous clubs world-wide whose history is truly inspiring and determined by religous or ethical ethos. Anyone with an interest in Celtic should research the club and then it becomes apparent why Celtic is described as "More than just a football club", Celtic is one of the football worlds pearls, an institution whose contribution to "The beautiful game" is unrivaled by all but a very select few. "A grand old team" indeed, thanks for the article. **Brianbhoy.** Celtic Park has become legendary for its atmosphere, comfortably topping a BBC poll to find Britain's favourite sporting venue. www.fifa.com/classicfootball/clubs

908. IN THE MID 1890's Sheffield United tried to sign **Willie Maley** and also offered him a part time job as an accountant. Fortunately for Celtic he declined the offer.

909. " HOW DO you spell Euphemia?" **Fergus McCann** said to Ann Lennon's mum, who had chapped his car window outside Celtic Park and asked him for an autograph. Fergus then signed his Celtic View with some nice words and gave it to her : " All the best Euphemia from all at Celtic Park and Fergus McCann. ". This made her day.

910. "I THANK GOD for bringing me here today". **Jorge Cadete** after
he scored on his debut against Aberdeen on April Fools day 1996.
He had signed on 23 February, but delays with his registration in
the SFA meant he had five weeks of frustration.

911. "THE LEVEL OF support required by Celtic at this time was not
obtainable from them." **Fergus McCann** in 1994 severs Celtic's
business with the Bank of Scotland after Celtic almost went bank-
rupt.

912. " I DON'T want to give them one thin dime " **Fergus McCann**
when he started financial talks with the old Celtic Board

913. " AFTER THE game when we beat Ajax 2-1 in Amsterdam, I went
into the Ajax dressing room and asked every player if they would
swap jerseys. Not one person spoke to me. As I turned to walk out,
I heard a voice " hey McCluskey " and it was the world's greatest
player, Johan Cruyff, on the treatment table receiving a leg massage and smoking a cigarette. He gave me his jersey." **George
McCluskey**, who scored a goal in that game.

914. ONE HALF OF Glasgow just don't like you, and the other half think
they own you. **Tommy Burns**

915. " I DON'T want my house burned down". Joked Celtic masseur
Jimmy Steel when Graeme Souness tried to sign him for Rangers.
Jimmy was well respected by everyone in football because of his
wonderful personality, humour, and kindness to everyone. Jimmy
served Celtic for over forty years.

916. **JOCK WEIR** HAS a place in Celtic's history because of the hat
trick he scored against Dundee in 1948 when Celtic were almost
relegated. A few years later he was with Celtic on their tour of
America. Celtic played German team Eintracht Frankfurt for the
Schaeffer Trophy when fighting broke out in the crowd, and then

on the pitch. Jock turned to his marker and told him, " I was paid two bob a day during the war to kill big bastards like you".

917. THERE IS A story that Fergus McCann was taking his daily walk around Celtic Park and looked up at the flag pole and noticed the Tricolour was not flying. " Where is the flag?" asked Fergus. " " It is at the laundry " was the reply. " Please get another tricolour. Celtic Park is never to be without the flag"

918. IN THE SUMMER of 1980, **Tommy Burns** married Rosemary in Saint Francis church in the Gorbals. Legend has it that the organist played the "Celtic Song" as the happy couple came down the aisle.

919. JOCK STEIN WOULD loved being a manager today. Can you imagine him doing all those live interviews straight after the games with those young whipper snapper interviewers who always try to catch out managers with smart questions.? They would have been scared stiff to do an interview with Big Jock. The motto of the BBC is to enrich people's lives with programmes that "*inform, educate* and *entertain.*"   Big Jock did all three when he talked about Celtic. **Pub football expert**

920. STRIKERS CAN GO months without scoring a goal. Football is a game played with the mind, not with the feet. With confidence a player can do wonders, but without it he will be eaten alive at Celtic Park. Celtic players must all be mentally tough as nuts. The big Greek bhoy will come good. Pub Expert talking about striker **Giorgios Samaras** who went 3 months without scoring

921. ON 16 APRIL 1904 Celtic beat Ranger 3-2 in the Scottish Cup Final after being 2 goals down. Jimmy Quinn scored a hat trick which put him into Celtic folklore. Manager **Willie Maley** summed up the victory by saying: " The enthusiasm of youth, and the never say die spirit to conquer, coupled with harmony in execution, sent Celtic rioting home to a wonderful victory".

922. PICTURE THE SCENE: it is the last few minutes of the second leg of the European Cup semi final in Prague when Celtic are playing Dukla Prague. The fans are shouting at the referee to blow the final whistle. " no fur ma sake, no fur God's sake, but for fxxx sake!" Line from the play " **On our Way to Lisbon**" written by Patrick Prior

923. " WHEN I was seven, there was a Celtic scout watching one of our matches, and he decided he would like to sign the wee 'boy' in the No 7 shirt on an 'S' [schoolboy] form. That was me, of course. Our coach said to him, 'But, look, she's a wee lassie'. I was devastated. I was in tears. I could not understand why I couldn't sign on. I said, 'Why can a girl not play for Celtic?'. When you're seven years old you don't know about these things. When you're that age you think you can play for Celtic. But I kind of lived my dream, because I decided I was going to be a professional foot-baller." **Rose Reilly**, Scotland's greatest woman footballer. She played most of her career in the Italian woman's league. In 1983 in front of a 90,000 crowd in Peking, she was the captain of the Italian women's team who beat the USA 3-1 in the World Cup final. She scored a goal from 40 yards in that game.

924. HE CAN TELL his grandchildren about it. He will take it to his grave. It was no fluke. You can't pull someone out of the stand to do that. Naka can do that six or seven times out of ten. Celtic's **John Hartson** talking about the famous free kick Nakamura scored against Manchester United at Celtic Park on 21 November 2006. Celtic won 1-0.

925. " WHY DO you think you always have to score good goals? " **Jock Stein**. A goal is a goal no matter how ugly or scrambled it is.

926. SANDY MCMAHON PLAYED in the first Celtic team to win the Scottish Cup in 1893. He scored twice. He had a good record in the Scottish Cup and scored 45 goals in 43 games. His great grand-

son, Matt McCombe lives in Las Vegas, and in the late 1990's he donated two of Sandy's medals and caps to the Celtic museum.

927. THE DISAPPOINTMENTS ARE important because they make the achievements more enjoyable. People used to say to me " it must have been easy during the nine-in-a-row sequence after you won the first few titles." I would tell them " no, it gets harder every year. The more succesful you are, the harder people try to stop you". **Billy McNeill**

928. **ALEC COLLINS** WAS a right-back in the very early days of Celtic. He played right back in September 1888 in Celtic's first ever Cup Final (Glasgow Exhibition Cup) which Celtic lost 2-0 to Cowlairs. Fifty years later in the 1930's he said footballers of the day were a namby pamby lot! He recalled that players of his era had to work, as well as play. In his case he worked from 6 o'clock in the morning until five thirty in the evening at the railway works.

929. THE RIO FERGUS McCann Celtic Supporters Club, is based in Rio de Janeiro, Brasil. The Bhoys From Brasil received a very welcoming and encouraging letter of support from His Bunnetness (Fergus McCann) giving his support for the founding of the supporters club in 2006. They do a lot of work for local charities.

930. CELTIC FANS NEVER lost their sense of humour even in the dark days of the early 1990's. They would sing the tune from the Monty Python film " The Life of Brian". " Always look on the Bright Side of Life. Do doo, do doo do doo do doo. Always look on the Bright side of Life, Do doo, do doo do doo do doo.

931. **JIMMY QUINN** WAS the first Celtic player to score over 200 goals.

932. JOCK STEIN WAS a brilliant judge of strikers, and most of them were small in size. But they were all hard. Joe McBride and Willie Wallace were ferocious fighters and could take of themselves in the penalty area. **Bobby Murdoch.**

933. **BOBBY TEMPLETON** WAS Scotland's first showman of football. He was the Ronaldo of his day. He signed for Celtic in 1906. He was a full time professional who knew his financial worth – football was not a hobby to him, but it was his profession. He was one of the first players to negotiate being paid during the close season (May, June, July). Other players had to return to a job during those months to earn money to put food on the family table. Once he left Celtic he had various business interests. He died in 1919 aged 41 years old of heart failure while lacing up his boots to play a Sunday morning game of football.

934. " MUR –DOCK". The answer a foreign journalist gave when he was asked to sum up the Celtic team of the Lisbon era. **Bobby Murdoch** was the man who made the team tick.

935. "I KNOW YOU were sick about missing the last final (in Lisbon), but if you do well for me tonight and we reach the final, you'll definitely play." **Jock Stein** to John Hughes before the European Cup semi final in 1970 against Leeds. Yogi went out and scored in the 2-1 victory over Leeds that night.

936. " MARTIN WALKS on water, Dick disnae ". Graffiti on a wall in Glasgow comparing Celtic manager Martin O'Neill to Rangers manager Dick Advocaat, who spent millions of pounds. Celtic won the treble that season 2000/2001. Dick was caught for speeding on his way to Rangers training ground Murray Park that season and when questioned by the police answered "I'll do anything for 3 points".

937. " OH CRAIG, the problem with you is that all your brains are in your head." Celtic fan shouts to Lisbon Lion **Jim Craig** after a bad pass. Jim had just sat his final dentistry exams at University.

938. I WOULD HAVE booted it and seen if the referee would give us another toss. **Jock Stein** in response to a question from his captain Billy McNeill " what would you have done if the coin came down

tails?" Billy had just guessed correctly "heads" when the referee tossed the coin after Celtic drew 3-3 on aggregate with Benfica in a European Cup game in 1969. In the 1960's drawn games were decided by the toss of a coin.

939. 'AT LEAST YOU'LL be going home with a runners-up medal'. Celtic's **Lou Macari** to Partick Thistle's **John Hansen** before the the League Cup in 1971, that Thistle won 4-1. " He wasn't being mischievous, he was being kind" said John. " Of course, we'd no chance. Some of us were full-timers, but goalie Alan Rough had just qualified as an electrician, centre-half Jackie Campbell was a draughtsman, striker Frank Coulston was a PE teacher, and teenage winger Denis McQuade was studying Classics at Glasgow Uni. The year before most of us had been playing for Thistle re-serves against Glasgow Police and Glasgow Transport. I mean, how could I even be thinking about winning the cup when I had the job of marking wee Jinky Johnstone? What a player and such a nice guy you could never bring yourself to kick him. Whenever you played against Jimmy he kept up a running conversation. 'OK, big yin, try harder to get the ball this time' he'd say. 'Jimmy,' I'd plead, 'just go past me and cross the ball, will you?' But no, he'd go past, then double back to beat you again. . . and just maybe a third time."

940. " FETCH A polis man, Everton's getting murdered" shout from a Celtic supporter before the Empire Exhibition Cup final in 1938. Celtic won 1-0 with a goal from **Johnny Crum** in extra time. It was a tough game and the score was 0-0 after 90 minutes.

941. GOALKEEPER **PETER LATCHFORD** won three Scottish Cup win-ners medals. (Airdrie 3-1 in 1975: Rangers 1-0 in 1977: Rangers 1-0 in 1980). He played 272 games for Celtic. His last game was in May 1987 against Rangers in the Glasgow Cup final, and Lex Baillie scored an own goal past Peter.

942. "WHAT A PLAYER you might have been Bertie if you had two feet."
Jock Stein used to say to **Bertie Auld** who was all left foot. Bertie
used to reply " Boss, when you have a left peg like mine, you don't
need a right foot!"

943. THE CELTIC v East Fife Scottish Cup Final in 1927 was the first
match to be broadcast on the radio. A small number of people
in the country owned a radio at that time. A few ice cream par-
lours in Methil and Leven had a radio with a speaker, and people
flocked to hear the game. Celtic won 3-1. The goals were scored
by McLean, Connolly and Robertson (og).

944. ONLY TWO GOALS have ever been scored direct from a free kick in
Scottish Cup Finals. Is this history in the making? TV commentator Archie MacPherson just before Celtic's **Davie Provan** ran
up to take a free kick against Dundee United in the 1985 Scottish
Cup Final. Davie curled a great goal into the top of the net.

945. AT THE AGM in 1997 a Shareholder stood up and said to **Fergus
McCann:** "I tell you that 90% of the people here are not interested in business. They are interested only in the playing side of
things." Fergus replied "I tell you that without the business, there
would be no club - and NO team."

946. **JOCK STEIN** WOULD always defend his players from journalists. "
You cannot criticise a player when he is outnumbered two to one
every time he has the ball."

947. " WATCH HIM and the way he goes about the game. Nobody
knows more than Bobby Murdoch about how best to get the ball
from where it is, to that place where you can do some damage in
the quickest and most economical way. He's brilliant at that." **Jock
Stein** talking about Bobby Murdoch. He could change a game
with one pass.

948. SOME PEOPLE WILL say it is madness for me to take this job. I'm ready to invest in madness. **Martin O'Neill** on the day he became manager at Celtic.

949. " THE GROUND was like a furnace, the dressing-room conditions disgraceful, and the referee had no control whatever." Celtic manager **Willie Maley** talking after the game against Pawtucket Rangers at Rhode Island during Celtic's North America tour in 1931. The 'friendly' turned into a roughhouse affair and Celtic required a police escort at time-up. This was Celtic's first ever tour of the USA and it was during the Great Depression. Times were hard, and in the game against Montreal Carsteel, Peter Scarff scored five goals while wearing a green dress shirt because there weren't enough Hoops strips to go around the team. The football on this tour was tough: in the game against Hakoah All-Stars, Jimmy McGrory had his jaw smashed, and Charlie Napier and Peter Scarff were sent off along with two Hakoah players. Football in the 1930's was not for soft players.

950. " WHERE THE hell is the cup?" **Jimmy McGrory** on stepping off the train Toronto's Union Station in 1951. Celtic were on their North America tour and had brought along the Scottish Cup that they had just won. Nobody could find it, but eventually a young Scottish lad, taking his holidays to follow his favourite team, said "Mr McGrory here it is" much to Jimmy's relief. Since then the Scottish Cup has never again been allowed out of Scotland.

951. IN 1957 CELTIC made a trip to North America aboard Cunard's ship RMS Mauritania. A menu from the trip, autographed by the Celtic team, was sold on EBay for £112 in March 2004. The seller described the menu as: "Cunard's RMS Mauritania Menu, dated Monday May 13th 1957, for a Gala Dinner held on board." The back of the menu has been autographed by the players and management of Celtic FC, which include Robert Kelly (Chairman),

Jimmy McGrory (Manager), Sean Fallon, Duncan MacKay, John Donnelly, Eric Smith, Charlie Tully and Bertie Peacock.

952. In 1973 CELTIC beat Rangers 3-1 in the semi final of the League Cup at Hampden. It was pouring with rain. **Harry Hood** scored the perfect hat trick – left foot, right foot, and a header. The Celtic fans were in full song: " Singin' in The Rain", " Harry Hood Superstar – How many goals have you scored so far?" and Harry Harry Harry Hood, half the price and twice as Good. " (as opposed to Rangers big name signing Colin Stein who had cost double the money of Harry). Harry also scored a fourth goal that night but the referee made a bad decision and disallowed it.

953. In 1966 JOCK Stein took Celtic on a tour of North America and Bermuda. This was the tour that made the Lisbon Lions so close as players and friends. In eleven matches played, Celtic scored 47 goals and conceded only 6. **Bobby Lennox** later said: "with that impressive record behind us we looked forward to 1966-7 with confidence, yet not realizing that for all of us the greatest season of our lives was about to dawn."

954. THE CELTIC TOUR of America and Canada in 1968 was more of a holiday than work for the players. Celtic's doctor, **John Fitzsimmons**, described the journey, "Splendidly attired in green club blazers and grey flannels our party of 16 players and five officials board the plane at Prestwick Airport that is to take us to New York on the first stage of our Transatlantic tour." Over the next few days the Celtic party relaxed and took advantage of all that Miami had to offer. Colour television, which was a new technology with multiple channels, deep sea fishing, and golf were among the players favourites. The final match of the tour was against Nececa of Mexico in Mexico City. Because of the difference in altitude, some of the players had difficulty breathing properly and it affected the players during the match. At half-time Celtic were 3-1 down, Billy McNeill scored Celtic's goal with a

header. During the half-time break the players were given oxygen and played better in the second half – Willie Wallace scored to make the final score 3-2 to Nececa.

955. Dr. Roddy MacDonald moved to Celtic in 1999 to take over medical team at Celtic Park. Prior to this he had worked in war torn Afghanistan with charity organisation Medecins Sans Frontiers. Roddy was a big Celtic fan and could be seen celebrating in the dugout when Celtic scored. One of his most important roles is the medical check on any player Celtic are about to sign. It does not matter what the manager or Chief Executive say, but if Dr.Roddy says a player is not fit for employment, then Celtic will not sign him.

956. In 1972 **Jock Stein** took the Celtic team on a break to Bermuda after winning the 7th Scottish League Championship in a row. Big Jock said, "The players deserved this break. They have worked hard for it all season." In the second match against Pembroke, Celtic won 8-1. But Billy McNeill was sent off for a comment he made to the referee.

957. " There is no excuse for a professional footballer not to be 100% fit." **Jock Stein** who disliked alcohol.

958. Cardinal Winning studied Canon Law in Rome. He worked hard, becoming fluent in Italian, and perfecting his Latin by translating reports of Celtic's football matches into the language. In later years he attended almost every home game at CelticPark. But he avoided "Old Firm" matches, because he disapproved of the naked sectarianism on show.

959. **Bobby Lennox** was so quick and must hold the world record for having his goals disallowed because linesmen could not keep up with him. They needed TV action replays but they had not been invented yet. The wee buzz bomb must have been born offside. **Pub football expert**

960. FOR CELTIC FANS who are too young to have watched the Lisbon Lions, or to have stood in The Jungle and cheered the team onto 9 league titles in a row, then they must rely on the stories from their fathers, uncles, older brothers, and granddads to learn about the dribbling skills of Jimmy Johnstone, the vision and passing of Bobby Murdoch, the cavalier spirit of Tommy Gemmell, and the speed of Bobby Lennox. As **Bertie Auld** said, "It was not a question of were you going to win. In those days it was how many goals are you going to win by." **Pub football expert**

961. EVERYBODY WAS VERY excited, no doubt about it. If you look at pictures of people leaving for this game, they were going dressed in suits and collars and ties. A working man in Glasgow wouldn't wear a collar and tie unless he was either going to church on Sunday or going to something special like a wedding or a funeral. These guys went to that game dressed in collars and ties because it really was something special. Celtic fan **Bernie Boyle** talking about Lisbon in 1967.

962. SINCE I BECAME Chief Executive in 1994 I have had big changes in my life. I am not used to being in the public eye and it is quite an adjustment. I didn't realise that it would be so intense, that I would have no privacy, people following me. You have to change your phone number and all that stuff. It's a bit difficult but nevertheless I don't mind. As long as the team are doing well they'll keep away from me and they don't care who I am. **Fergus McCann**.

963. I WAS BORN on April 4, 1986, in Rutherglen, Glasgow, and I have lived in Glasgow all my life. One of my earliest memories is of kicking a ball about with my dad, John, when I was about six, but I wasn't really interested in it that much. Then, when I was eight, one of my mates was starting up with Busby Boys' Club, who played about ten minutes away from my home on the south side of Glasgow, and he asked me to go along with him. I went along and found that I really enjoyed it straightaway. We played

seven-a-sides and I played in midfield. **Aiden McGeady**. www. aidenmcgeadyofficialwebsite.com

964. IN THE 1990's Celtic had the " 3 Amigos" playing for them 'Pierre Van Hooijdonk', Jorge Cadette and Paolo di Canio. But in the 1930's Celtic had "The Terrible Trio", - **Crum, Divers and Macdonald** – who revolutionised football by their constant interchanging of position and quick feet. Defenders were not used to playing against players like this.

965. HOW CAN I decide between Lisbon and the 7-1 game against Rangers? Winning the European Cup was wonderful, but I am going for the 7-1 match as we were the underdogs but at the end of the day Rangers were not even at the races. **James Flaherty** speaking in 1994. He had been watching Celtic for the past 74 years and had seen some great games in Celtic's history.

966. FOOTBALL WAS THE greatest part of our lives, just like the boys from Brazil and Spain. They lived in poverty, like us, and that's where all the great players came from - the street. **Jimmy Johnstone**

967. WHEN CELTIC BEAT Boavista in the semi final of the UEFA Cup 2003, the players were given a huge cheer by the fans when they arrived in the departure lounge of Oporto airport later that night. The Jolly Green Giant, **Bobo Balde**, was so happy that he jumped into a group of Celtic supporters punching the air in delight.

968. I DOUBT IF I will ever forget the scenes at Oporto airport after the Boavista game. The fans spend a lot of money to come and cheer us on, behave impeccably, and I can assure you it is appreciated in the dressing room. **Martin O'Neill**

969. IN THE 1967 European Cup Final in Lisbon all 5 of the Celtic forward line in that game had been wingers at some stage of their football careers – Johnstone, Wallace, Chalmers, Auld and Lennox.

970. KENNY DALGLISH WAS a great player. He had eyes in the back of his head. How did he always know who was behind him? **Billy Connolly**

971. WHEN CELTIC BEAT Rangers 7-1 in the League Cup final in 1957, Rangers only scored their goal when Celtic were down to 10 men. **Bobby Evans** was off the field receiving treatment for an injury.

972. ANDY GORAM THE former Rangers is obviously not a Celtic fan, but he was kind enough to send me a fax after I was injured. **Henrik Larsson** after his horror leg break against Olympique Lyonnais in 1999.

973. IN THE WORLD Club Championship game against Racing Club in Montevideo in 1967, four of the Celtic forwards were sent off. Johnstone, Lennox, Hughes and Auld. (although Bertie refused to leave the field) Only Willie Wallace was not sent for an early bath.

974. CELTIC HAVE ALWAYS had an attacking style of football. Here is a list of the players who were the top scores in the first hundred years. Season 1888-89 Willie Groves (10): 1890-91 Peter Dowds (17): 1891-92 Sandy McMahon (25): 1892-93 Sandy McMahon (19): 1893-94 Sandy McMahon (30): 1894-95 Sandy McMahon (9): 1895-96 Allan Martin (18): 1896-97 Sandy McMahon (10): 1897-98 George Allan (16): 1898-99 Sandy McMahon (21): 1899-1900 Jack Bell and Sandy McMahon (12 each): 1900-01 Johnny Campbell and Sandy McMahon (13 each): 1901-02 Johnny Campbell (12): 1902-03 Johnny Campbell (15): 1903-04 Jimmy Quinn (15): 1904-05 Jimmy Quinn (21): 1905-06 Jimmy Quinn (21): 1906-07 Jimmy Quinn (30): 1907-08 Jimmy Quinn (20): 1908-09 Jimmy Quinn (29): 1909-10 Jimmy Quinn (28): 1910-11 Jimmy Quinn (17): 1911-12 Jimmy Quinn (11): 1912-13 Jimmy Quinn (11): 1913-14 Patsy Gallacher (24): 1914-15 Jimmy McColl (25): 1915-16 Jimmy McColl (34): 1916-17 Jimmy McColl (24):

1917-18 Patsy Gallacher (17): 1918-19 Jimmy McColl 17): 1919-20 Tommy McInally (30): 1920-21 Tommy McInally (30): 1921-22 Joe Cassidy and Tommy McInally (18 each): 1922-23 Joe Cassidy (32): 1923-24 Joe Cassidy (25): 1924-25 Jimmy McGrory (28): 1925-26 Jimmy McGrory (42): 1926-27 Jimmy McGrory (57): 1927-28 Jimmy McGrory (53): 1928-29 Jimmy McGrory (31): 1929-30 Jimmy McGrory (35): 1930-31 Jimmy McGrory (44): 1931-32 Jimmy McGrory (28): 1932-33 Jimmy McGrory (30); 1933-34 Frank O'Donnell (27): 1934-35 Jimmy McGrory (20): 1935-36 Jimmy McGrory (50): 1936-37 Jimmy McGrory (26): 1937-38 Johnny Crum (25): 1938-39 John Divers (21): 1939-40 Johnny Crum (2): 1946-47 Tommy Kiernan (17): 1947-48 Johnny Paton (10): 1948-49 Jackie Gallacher (22): 1949-50 John McPhail (21): 1950-51 John McPhail (28): 1951-52 Bobby Collins (13): 1952-53 John McGrory and Bertie Peacock (11): 1953-54 Neil Mochan (25): 1954-55 Jimmy Walsh (24): 1955-56 Neil Mochan (20): 1956-57 Billy McPhail (17): 1957-58 Sammy Wilson (32): 1958-59 John Colrain (16): 1959-60 Neil Mochan (22): 1960-61 Steve Chalmers (26): 1961-62 John Hughes (26): 1962-63 John Hughes (21): 1963-64 Steve Chalmers (38): 1964-65 Steve Chalmers (26): 1965-66 Joe McBride (43): 1966-67 Steve Chalmers (36): 1967-68 Bobby Lennox (41): 1968-69 Willie Wallace (34): 1969-70 Willie Wallace (24): 1970-71 Harry Hood (33): 1971-72 Dixie Deans (27): 1972-73 Kenny Dalglish (41): 1973-74 Dixie Deans (33): 1974-75 Paul Wilson (22): 1975-76 Kenny Dalglish (32): 1976-77 Kenny Dalglish (26): 1977-78 Joe Craig (16): 1978-79 Tom McAdam (13): 1979-80 Johnny Doyle (15): 1980-81 Frank McGarvey (29): 1981-82 George McCluskey (25): 1982-83 Charlie Nicholas (48): 1983-84 Brian McClair (31): 1984-85 Brian McClair (23): 1985-86 Brian McClair (26): 1986-87 Brian McClair (41): 1987-88 Andy Walker (32): 1988-89 Mark McGhee (19).

975. BE POSITIVE, BUT prepare for life after football while you are enjoying football. That means getting an education, because if you come out the game in your 30s, if you are lucky enough to play that long, even if you are a multi-millionaire, you will still hopefully have another 40 years ahead of you. So you need your education to protect your money and open up doors within media and business. Follow your dream, enjoy your football, but prepare for life afterwards along the way because your playing career will be like a click of your fingers, it comes and goes so quickly. Celtic centre half **Paul Elliot** gives some advise to young boys to follow their dream if they want to be a footballer.

976. "I THINK YOU'RE very hard on that wee fellow." **Jock Stein's** mum rebuked him for sometimes being too tough on Jimmy Johnstone.!

977. THERE ARE STILL a lot of rascals in the game. It is a pity that the authorities (FIFA) have turned a blind eye to it. I am perfectly happy with the fact that football agents do not like dealing with me. You have to fight fire with fire at times. **Fergus McCann**

978. I KNOW THAT I would not have the brains to do it, but I would like to be a doctor.They do a worthwhile job and I am sure it would be interesting. Or even a surgeon, a plastic surgeon would be best, then I could give Peter Grant a much needed facelift! Celtic player **Tommy Burns** when asked what job he would have liked if he was not a footballer.

979. **BOBBY EVANS** PLAYED over 500 games for Celtic. He was known for his red hair, jersey outside his shorts, and giving 100% effort in every game he played. He was never ordered off and only booked three times in his long career, which is remarkable for someone who played in the half back position. He had strong sporting principles which is a wonderful gift for any Celtic player.

980. Jock Stein had asked Father Bertie O'Regan to say a mass to the team before we played Inter Milan in the European Cup Final. The mass was held in a convent opposite our hotel to celebrate the feast of Corpus Christi. But Father O'Regan had no altar boy to assist, so our assistant manager Sean Fallon stepped in! **John Clark**

981. I've got three children to look after and have seven dogs to walk, so I am kept busy away from football. We also have two pigs, a couple of goats, and some cats. When I finish playing I'd like to settle down in the country and keep lots of animals. **Chris Sutton.**

982. " Celtic's first sod of turf: It was in this field on the 10th day of April 1995 that the first sod of turf for the new Celtic Park Glasgow was cut." – This plaque is displayed at the field in Mullachdubh, Rosses in Donegal. The local Celtic Supporters cut the sod, took it Celtic Park, and placed in the centre circle. Fergus McCann gave permission and thanked the supporters for their actions as he thought it was important to have a link to Ireland.

983. " When they come to write the history of Celtic in 2050 it will universally be acknowledged that the two greatest servants of all time were Jock Stein and Fergus McCann." **Jock Brown**

984. Its in my blood and at the end of the day a 300 mile round trip doesn't matter. Celtic fan **Scott Thoars** who travels from Aberdeen for every home game.

985. I was convinced that Brian would score goals with Celtic, but I remember a lot of people were questioning why I signed him from Motherwell. Celtic manager Billy McNeill talking about **Brian McClair**, who scored an incredible 121 goals in 142 games for Celtic.

986. Henrik Larsson knows he can change a game with one moment of magic. He is always calm in his mind during the 90 minutes even if things are not going well. He is the best player I have

worked with in 25 years, and that includes players like Dalglish,
Nicholas and McAvennie. **Tommy Burns**

987. " I've seen more running off the ball running playing Subbuteo".
Fan shouted to Celtic mid field player **Dom Sullivan**.

988. In 1955 **Willie Fernie** scored five goals against Queen of the
South. The referee disallowed the first three, so Willie walked the
ball into the net for the next two and looked at the referee to check
that they were good goals.

989. I don't know what the hell you are celebrating – you had nothing to be proud of. It wasn't enough to go through, we had to go
through with style. Celtic chairman to captain **Billy McNeill** in
Lisbon in 1969 after Celtic had "beat" Benfica on the toss of a coin
after a 3-3 draw on aggregate. The game did not finish until near
midnight, and and once back in the hotel the players had a wee
party. Unfortunately they woke up the chairman and Billy had to
go and apologise to him.

990. After a game I like to give big Frank Cairney a phone and ask
him about the match and my performance. Frank was my manager at Celtic Boys Club, is my mentor and I value his comments.
Charlie Nicholas

991. Peter Grant is a walking encyclopaedia on the singer Tom Jones
and loves imitating him, especially at our nights out. I remember
at one Christmas party for the players and our wives that he vol-
unteered to entertain us. He gave us The Green Green Grass of
Home right through to My My My Delilah. **Paul McStay**

992. It was four years before I watched a tape of the game. I don't know
why that was. The wife and kids were out one day and I had the
house to myself. I set up the film and watched every kick of the
European Cup Final. What struck me most was the intensity of
Celtic's technical play. The movement off the ball, the passing and

possession, the structure of play was superb. It was a delight to watch. The national stadium in Lisbon was a breathtaking tree-fringed amphitheatre, and it felt like you had to step down into the bowl, 100ft to get to the pitch. When we emerged we were met with an incredible sight. The whole stadium was a sea of green and white, flags, banners and scarves from all corners of Scotland. A wall of noise and tension. **Bertie Auld** talking about the 25 May 1967.

993. TONY TOLD ME that when he came to play against Celtic with Hibernian (when he was their manager), he used to work with his team all week in training on ways not to stop Henrik Larsson or Chris Sutton, but ways on stopping me. That's what he thought of me as a player at Celtic, but when I went to West Brom I was 32 and not the same player. He had the decency to say to me that although I had 18 months left on my deal I would not play. **John Hartson** talking about Tony Mowbray, ex Celtic centre half, ex manager of Hibs, and ex manager of West Bromich Albion.

994. " BEING BORN 100 years to the day after Celtic played their first official game, there was no doubt that I would grow up to become a true follower of Celtic Football club. I have had many great days and nights watching the bold bhoys in action as well as some terrible memories. But one of those great nights of recent times was the last game of the 2007/08 season when the league was to be decided on a Thursday night. The bold Celtic had a tough game away to Dundee United and the Gers were facing a hard task at Pittodrie against Aberdeen. Both games started at the same time and it was a tense match in both games. Then as soon as Miller scored for Aberdeen and Big Jan for Celtic, I knew we had done it. I watched the game in the Saints and Sinners pub in Bellshill (big Tim shop) and the atmosphere was electric. We piled out onto the street after the game to have a bit of rowdy with the Crown Bar. (big Rangers pub). We then started a Huddle around the traffic lights at the Bellshill Cross. Winning the title any season is

an amazing feeling, but the atmosphere and events that took place that night made it a little bit special.". **Nick Campbell**

995. JACKIE MCNAMARA (senior) was nick named " Boris" by his colleagues because he was a Communist. When he first signed for Celtic Jock Stein said " Jackie could be as good as if not better than Dalglish. He has all the skills, but is a slow developer "

996. WHEN CELTIC PLAYERS trained at Barrowfield in London Road, every morning at 10 o'clock when training started local youths used start a fire and burn tyres and black smoke used drift across the park as we started our running. We would be coughing and our lungs were choking, but they waved at us as they ran away. **Peter Grant.**

997. " WE COULD have played without a referee, or even a ball." **Willie Wallace** after the Battle of Montevidio against Racing Club. One of the most brutal games Celtic have ever been involved in.

998. FERGUS MCCANN WAS not a man for regrets, but he wished that he had met **Dr. Jo Venglos** long before he became manager of Celtic. Dr.Jo knew the value of a good footballer, and in his short time at Celtic brought in the magnificent Lubo Moravcik and recommended Stan Petrov. He got value for the money that he spent.

999. WHAT AN AMAZING 10 days I had at the Celtic Supporters convention in Las Vegas in June 2009. Let me share a story with you. Last New Year we watched the Rangers game at the Cheers Bar in Sydney. I was wearing a Celtic Santa Hat, and noticed these two lassies wearing the Hoops with Vegas 07 on the back of their jerseys. So I went over and talked to them, and told them I had been there as well and was going again this year. They were also going again, but only after a few more months backpacking around Australia. One of them wanted my Celtic Santa Hat, so I said only on the condition that I get it back in Las Vegas, which she agreed to. I went up to the Celtic Lounge on the night it opened in Vegas

2009 , and lo and behold I saw them sitting at the table !! I went over and said, "Where's my Santa hat". She looked up and recognised me and told me that she had just told her family and friends at the table 5 minutes before about the hat. Yes she had brought the hat, and she nipped off to her room and got it and gave it back to me. You might have saw them walking around Vegas wearing the Aussie corked hats. Can' t wait for Vegas 2011, which no doubt the guys on the committee started organising whilst the current one was still in progress. **Brian McAvoy Sydney City CSC.**

1000. " IN 1995/96 I went back to Glasgow and I met up with Bobby Murdoch, Bertie Auld, and Willie O'Neil at Bairds Bar on a Sunday morning at 9.30 (shutters doon). We were arranging to bring them out to visit South Africa and we just had to finalise a few things. When we had finished the meeting, I jokingly said to Bobby (I worshipped the ground he walked on. He was my all time favourite Celtic man)   "Hey Bobby now that were finished wi' the meeting lets just pop up to Celtic Park and take some photos ? It was meant as a joke, but Bobby just looked it meand said " OK Bill Let's go". I thought he was having me on! Next minute Bobby is taking me through the whole of Celtic Park, dressing room, board room, and even the referees wee change room. And then he took me out on to the CENTRE of the field. My most treasured photo is me and Bobby Murdoch standing together on the centre spot and me wearing my ancient silk Celtic scarf which I got for my 16th birthday, and my arm around a truly great man. The stadium was deserted except for 2 wee security blokes, and they were over the moon as well. I still have that photo on my desk in my office. And the greatest thing about the whole event is that I have it ALL on video. He was a great player, and a wonderful Human Being. P.S. I still have the box of Swan Vestas that Bobby had." **Bill** from Johannesburg, South Africa

" Big Jock Stein "song.

From a Lanarkshire town, came a man of great renown
Received an education, working under-ground
A Bevan Boy by trade, he worked and then he played
With Albion Rovers, he soon made the grade.

Because Jock Stein was a man, who was always in command
He didn't give a damn if you're a Billy or a Dan
He was the greatest ever seen, an he love the Bhoys in green
Jock Stein, was a Celtic fan.

For seven years or more, he made the Rovers roar
Then in 1950, he set out to explore
In Wales he settled down, with Llanelli Town
When he started full time football, a new lease of life was found.

Because Jock Stein was a man, who was always in command
He didn't give a damn if you're a Billy or a Dan
He was the greatest ever seen, an he love the Bhoys in green
Jock Stein, was a Celtic fan.

In 51 of late, a simple twist of fate
Brought him back to Scotland, and through the Parkhead gates
To captain he progressed, and he brought some great success
The double and the Coronation Cup with us he blessed.

Because Jock Stein was a man, who was always in command
He didn't give a damn if you're a Billy or a Dan
He was the greatest ever seen, an he love the Bhoys in green
Jock Stein, was a Celtic fan.

He crossed the Country wide, to a new Dunfermline side
He brought them Scottish glory, and a European pride

He moved to Hibs, and then to Paradise again
Soon the trophy's started coming again and again.

Because Jock Stein was a man, who was always in command
He didn't give a damn if you're a Billy or a Dan
He was the greatest ever seen, an he love the Bhoys in green
Jock Stein, was a Celtic fan.

13 years had gone, big Jock he move on
He won the European Cup in Lisbon in the sun
With 9 flags in a row, and silverware galore
And a whole generation was sad to see him go.

Because Jock Stein was a man, who was always in command
He didn't give a damn if you're a Billy or a Dan
He was the greatest ever seen, an he love the Bhoys in green
Jock Stein, was a Celtic fan.

To Elland Road was bound, but he never settled down
The Scottish fans were calling him back to his native town
Then in 1985, we last saw Jock alive
But he left us special memories right up until he died.

Because Jock Stein was a man, who was always in command
He didn't give a damn if you're a Billy or a Dan
He was the greatest ever seen, an he love the Bhoys in green
Jock Stein, was a Celtic fan.

source: website www.stoliverplunkettcsc.com

I love reading old books, programmes, and newspapers about the fascinating history of Celtic. I could spend hours doing this for fun! There are many dedicated people who know the history of Celtic in great detail; writers/historians like Pat Woods, David Potter, Eugene MacBride, Tom Campbell, Lisbon Lion Jim Craig, and many others. Their books are great reading and provide invaluable sources of information for all Celtic supporters. The internet is also a great source of Celtic information. I spent hours Googling across the world for quotes and notes.

I also want to thank Barry Hall for sharing his friend's (Michael Starrs) old case full of Celtic Views and fanzines that have been lying in his garden shed for years. It was fascinating reading. Also to Paul Cooney, Eddie McGuire, Paul McCormick, and Ann Lennon who helped provide some quotes.

Every pub has a football expert/philosopher who has wee gems of wisdom. In our local, old Willie comes out with some beauties after a few beers. He likes an argument now and then and is never wrong.

Some of the books I used for reference from my own book collection are listed below. These were all great sources of information and good bedtime reading.

One of my hobbies is reading books on Celtic. There are many dedicated people who know the history of Celtic in great detail; writers/historians like Pat Woods, David Potter, Eugene MacBride, Tom Campbell, Lisbon Lion Jim Craig, and many others. Their books are great reading and provide invaluable sources of information for Celtic supporters.

I also want to Thank my friend John McGuigan for sharing with me his scrap book of cuttings from the Lisbon Lion days. It was a treasure trove and unique collection. Also John Cassidy for sharing his collection of Celtic Views from the mid 1960's. It was fascinating reading.

Some of the books in my own library which were excellent sources of information when looking for information on Celtic quotes, notes and anecdotes were;

1. A Lion Looks Back by Jim Craig.
2. Rhapsody in Green by Tom Campbell and Pat Woods
3. Celtic's Paranoia – all in the mind? Tom Campbell
4. James "Dun" Hay – the story of a footballer by Roy Hay
5. The official little book of Celtic quotes and trivia by Douglas Russell
6. The little book of Celtic by Graham McColl
7. Celtic – the top 11 of everything by Steve Morgan
8. The Celtic football Miscellany by John White.
9. Celtic Triumphant by Ian Peebles
10. Bobby Murdoch, Different Class by David Potter
11. The Hoops Quiz Book by John White
12. The Glory and the Dream by Tom Campbell and Pat Woods
13. The Story of Celtic 1888-1978 by Gerald McNee
14. A Celtic A-Z by Tom Campbell and Pat Woods
15. Jock Stein biography by Archie Macpherson
16. Talking with Celts by Eugene MacBride
17. Celtic by Robert Kelly
18. Celtic football legends 1888-1938 by Stuart Marshall
19. Celtic My Team by Danny McGrain
20. Henrik Larsson – A season in Paradise by Mark Sylvester
21. Celtic in Europe – four decades of drama by Graham McColl
22. Celtic FC the 25 year record by Michael Robinson
23. Images of Sport – Celtic football club 1887-1967 by Tom Campbell and Pat Woods
24. Jungle Tales by John Quinn
25. The official Celtic annual 1992
26. Celtic – the Centenary edition by Ian Archer
27. Celtic fact file by Chris Mason
28. Fields of Green by Roddy Forsyth
29. Keep the Faith by Ron Mackenna and Carlos Alba
30. Playing for Celtic by Rodger Baillie
31. You are my Larsson by Mark Guidi and Ewing Grahame
32. Heroes are Forever – the life and times of Celtic legend Jimmy McGrory by John Cairney

33. Playing for Celtic number 2 by Rodger Baillie
34. Hail Cesar the autobiography Billy McNeill
35. Celtic Greats by Hugh Keevins
36. For Celtic and Scotland by Billy McNeill
37. A Million Miles for Celtic by Bobby Lennox
38. Walk on – Celtic since McCann by David Potter
39. Willie Maley the man who made Celtic by David Potter
40. Playing for Celtic number 15 by Rodger Baillie
41. Dalglish my autobiography
42. The Old Firm Joke book by Michael Munro
43. The Head Bhoys – Celtic's managers by Graham McColl
44. Soccer from the shoulder by Tommy Docherty
45. Back to Paradise by Billy McNeill
46. The story of the Celtic 1888-1938 by Willie Maley
47. The Celtic story by James E.Handley
48. Ten Days that shook Celtic by Tom Campbell
49. The Mighty Quinn by David Potter
50. Glasgow Celtic 1945-1970 by Tom Campbell
51. Passed to You by Charlie Tully.
52. Twists and Turns the Tommy Burns story by Hugh Keevins
53. Playing for Celtic number 18 by Rodger Baillie
54. Playing for Celtic number 16 by Rodger Baillie
55. The Celtic football companion by David Docherty
56. Playing for Celtic number 4 by Rodger Baillie
57. Not playing for Celtic another Paradise Lost by David Bennie
58. Lion Heart by Tommy Gemmell
59. The Big Shot by Tommy Gemmell
60. Sure it's a Grand Old team to play for by Ronnie Simpson
61. Celtic the official history by 1888-1995 by Graham McColl
62. An alphabet of the Celts by Eugene MacBride, Martin O'Connor and George Sheridan
63. Sack the Board – by Allan Caldwell
64. Fire in my Boots by Jimmy Johnstone
65. The Mighty Atom by David Potter
66. You can call me Stan by Stiliyan Petrov

97. Paradise Lost – David Hay/Ken Gallacher

98. Wee Barra – Bobby Collins – by David Saffer

99. Scoring: An Experts Guide by Frank McAvennie.

100. Hoopy Comes to Paradise by Maureen Hardie

101. The Little book of Celtic. By Graham Betts

102. The Best of the Celtic View

103. Celtic – a Complete Record 1888-1992. Paul Lunney

104. On their Way to Lisbon by Donald Montgomery

105. Celtic – the Encyclopaedia by Tom Campbell and George Sheridan

106. The Zen of Naka by Martin Greig

107. Scottish Football Hall of Fame – John Cairney

108. The Encyclopaedia of Scottish Football – David Potter and Phil H. Jones

109. The Lisbon Lions by Alex Gordon

110. Celtic in the League Cup by David Potter

111. The battle of Montevideo – Celtic under Siege by Brian Belton

112. Celtic First, Last, and Always by Paul Larkin

113. Celtic Year of Triumph (1967). Weekly News souvenir

114. Voices of the Old Firm by Stephen Walsh

115. Never turn the other Cheek by Paddy Crerand

116. Celtic Cult Heroes – David Potter

117. Now you know about Celtic: Bob Crampsey

118. Celtic FC The Ireland Connection – Brian McGurk

119. The Glory of the Green. – John Traynor and Douglas Russell

120. 100 Years of the Old Firm. Bill Murray

121. Celtic & Ireland in Song and Story by Raymond Daly and Derek Warfield

122. Over and Over – the story of Seville

123. My life in football. Gordon Strachan

124. In Sunshine or in Shadow. Danny McGrain

125. Tommy McInally – Celtic's Bad Bhoy? David Potter

About the Author

ROBERT WAS BORN and raised in Glasgow and has always loved football. He has been watching Celtic since he was 10 years old. He is lucky enough to have watched the Lisbon Lions. One of his earliest memories is the 1965 Scottish Cup Final when Celtic beat Dunfermline 3-2 with Billy McNeill scoring the winner. Robert was at school camp in Meigle, Perthshire that day with and his parents came to visit him. He still remembers all the Dads of the children listening to their transistor radios and the great roar when Celtic won! Other early memories include the 1967 Scottish Cup Final against Aberdeen at Hampden when he stood in the Celtic end with his dad and 120,000 other people as Celtic won 2-0. His first Old Firm game was in 1970 League Cup Final at Hampden in the rain when Celtic lost 1-0 to a Derek Johnstone header. The best Celtic game he has ever seen live was the UEFA Cup final in Seville in 2003. The best individual performance ever seen was Henrik Larsson in that final. Robert still gets excited every week when walking up Springfield Road to Celtic Park.